Essential Tests
for
IELTS

Academic Module

BY DONNA SCOVELL, VICKIE PASTELLAS & MAX KNOBEL

ADAMS & AUSTEN PRESS - SYDNEY, AUSTRALIA

Acknowledgements

The authors and publisher are grateful for permission to use copyright material. We would like to acknowledge the original sources of text material listed below. Permission has been sought to reproduce all material whose source could be identified. Information that will enable the publishers to rectify any error or omission in subsequent editions will be welcome.

We'd also like to thank UCLES for permission to reprint the IELTS bandscales and to reference material from 'The IELTS Handbook' accessible online at:

http//:www.ielts.org/handbook.htm

Practice Test 1: Reading Passage 2 was based on an article written by Mr B. Hesse at the Customer Technology Centre for SEQEB, Brisbane in 1989. Reading Passage 3 was based, in part, on information taken from the United Nations Environment Program website. Practice Test 2: Reading Passage 1 is an amalgamation created specifically for this publication. The authors used the names of real organisations and drew on published articles to create the text but facts have been changed so that the finished piece permits inferences to be drawn and questions framed to suit the fundamental purpose of this book (which is to give an understanding of the IELTS testing process). Practice Test 2: Reading Passage 2 is from the The Weekend Australian, Saturday 26 July 2003 "Anxious and Addicted" by Clare Pirani.

The facts set out as content in this text should not be relied on or quoted for any purpose except in the context of this book. The passages have been written with the express purpose of providing strategic guidelines for teachers and students in preparation for the IELTS test.

Permission was granted to reproduce the graphs and tables used in Writing Task 1, Practice Tests 1 and 2 by The English Tourism Council and The Office on Smoking and Health (U.S.). The illustration in Writing Task 1 Practice Test 4 was adapted from 'The Yachtsman's Emergency Handbook: The Complete Survival Manual' Hollander, Neil & Mertes, Harald. 1980. Angus & Robertson, U.S. These sources are detailed in the tests themselves.

Illustrations by Max Knobel, cover design by Roman Balla (roman.balla@bigpond.com), recording produced by Peter Whitford with assistance from International Casting Service, Sydney.

Special Thanks to

The authors would like to thank the following people for their help in reviewing and/or trialling the materials used in these tests: Christabel Lee, Terry Peck, Jill Schiffmann, Lisa Simpson, Jan Snowball, Ann Thompson, Ian McGregor, Embassy CES Australia, and the English Language Programs at Queensland University of Technology International College.

To our colleagues, students and friends who provided us with encouragement and support, we hope that you find these preparation tests helpful. And to the students who sit for IELTS tests all over the world, best of luck to you.

About the Authors

The authors have more than 40 years of combined experience teaching English to overseas students across a variety of sectors. In addition to teaching and preparing students for the IELTS test, much of their experience has revolved around writing programs for academic English and university preparation courses.

By the Authors

'404 Essential Tests for IELTS - Academic Module' International Edition:

Book:	ISBN 0 9751832 0 6
Cassettes(2):	ISBN 0 9751832 1 4 *
Book & Audio CDs(2):	ISBN 0 9751832 2 2
Study Guide:	ISBN 0 9751832 5 7
Study Guide Cassette:	ISBN 0 9751832 7 3
Study Guide & Audio CD:	ISBN 0 9751832 8 1

'404 Essential Tests for IELTS - General Training Module' International Edition:

Book:	ISBN 0 9751832 3 0
Cassettes(2):	ISBN 0 9751832 1 4 *
Book & Audio CDs(2):	ISBN 0 9751832 4 9
Study Guide:	ISBN 0 9751832 6 5
Study Guide Cassette:	ISBN 0 9751832 7 3
Study Guide & Audio CD:	ISBN 0 9751832 9 X

Published by Adams & Austen Press

'101 Helpful Hints for IELTS - Academic Module' International Edition:

Book:	ISBN 0 9587604 6 2
Cassette:	ISBN 0 9578980 0 2 *
Book & Audio CD(1):	ISBN 0 9578980 6 1

'101 Helpful Hints for IELTS - General Training Module' International Edition:

Book:	ISBN 0 9587604 9 7
Cassette:	ISBN 0 9578980 0 2 *
Book & Audio CD(1):	ISBN 0 9578980 9 6

'202 Useful Exercises for IELTS - International Edition'

Book:	ISBN 0 9587604 7 0
Cassette:	ISBN 0 9578980 1 0
Book & Audio CDs(2):	ISBN 0 9578980 7 X

'202 Useful Exercises for IELTS - Australasian Edition'

Book:	ISBN 0 9587604 5 4
Cassette:	ISBN 0 9578980 2 9
Book & Audio CDs(2):	ISBN 0 9578980 5 3

* the listening test is the same for both Modules of the test

Available Soon

'101 Helpful Hints Online Course for IELTS'

'303 The IELTS Room'
International Edition - Practice Book & Cassette/CD

'1001 Academic Words or IELTS'

First published in Sydney, Australia 2004

ISBN 0 9751832 0 6

Adams & Austen Press Pty. Ltd. A.B.N. 96 087 873 943
PO Box 509, Marrickville, New South Wales, Australia 1475
Tel: 612-9590-4469   Fax: 612-9590-4471
Email: aap@aapress.com.au   www.aapress.com.au

Printed and bound in Australia by Southwood Press, Marrickville, NSW.

9 8 7 6 5 4 3 2 1

FOREWORD

When Donna, Vickie and Max approached Adams & Austen Press last year with a manuscript that promised four complete practice tests for IELTS, we were initially cautious. Perhaps every teacher has a book inside them, and many have tried to write short tests at some time, but not everyone can write tests that are more than a superficial attempt at cloning a test such as IELTS.

Would these tests be, then, a mere presentation of a number of typical IELTS question types - as so many IELTS books on the market seem content to be these days? From the outset, our IELTS range of books has attempted to go much further than this, advising students what to do in no uncertain terms in order that they might improve; and not provide just another opportunity to 'take a test'.

It was, then, with pleasure and some relief that we sat down to discover a solid book of, yes, four complete and thoroughly trialled tests, with questions chosen judiciously and with a great deal of thought as to what was being tested - as is the case with the official IELTS tests. It was immediately apparent that the test material on offer was rigorously engaging, thought-provoking and entertaining at one and the same time.

Accompanying this work were two manuscripts for in-depth Study Guides to further unlock the secrets inside the tests.

In a word, the tests and the books were essential.

The 404 Essential Tests for IELTS.

Terry Peck
April 2004

CONTENTS

INTRODUCTION
Page

Listening Sub-test

Reading Sub-test

Writing Sub-test

Speaking Sub-test

CONTENTS continued

THE FOUR PRACTICE TESTS

APPENDICES

INTRODUCTION

Do you want to study at tertiary level in an English-speaking country?

Studying abroad is a very real alternative in the 21st century. Many more students than ever before, from countries all over the world, can access the world of tertiary education. It takes money for tuition; a commitment to succeed and an acceptable level of English.

If you have the first two requirements – this book will help you with the third. If your goal is to be accepted into a university or college in an English-speaking country, then read on.

What is IELTS?

No student will gain entry into any reputable tertiary institution in any English-speaking country unless his or her level of English proficiency is deemed adequate.

One of the few tests which is widely accepted for this purpose is IELTS – The International English Language Testing System – or as it is commonly known, the IELTS test.

IELTS is an excellent indicator of English language ability because it tests the four macro skills of listening, reading, writing and speaking. The reading and writing sections of the test have two different versions - General Training Module and the Academic Module. You will need to sit for the Academic Module of the IELTS test if you wish to do undergraduate or postgraduate study in an English-speaking country.

Even though it may help you to have a certain level of general knowledge before going into the test, the test itself does not require any specialized vocabulary or technical expertise. The correct answers can be found within the confines of the test and it is advisable for any student planning to take the test, to learn the skills needed to find the answers.

IELTS tests your English level but it is still a test and like any test, there are skills that can be learned and practised in order to achieve the best possible result. The result may decide your future. For each of the four different sections or modules of the test, a score is given from 0-9. These band scores are interpreted as follows:

Score	Description	Detailed description
9	**Expert User**	Has fully operational command of the language: appropriate, accurate and fluent with complete understanding.
8	**Very Good User**	Has fully operational command of the language with only occasional unsystematic inaccuracies and inappropriacies. Misunderstandings may occur in unfamiliar situations. Handles complex detailed argumentation well.
7	**Good User**	Has operational command of the language, though with occasional inaccuracies, inappropriacies and misunderstandings in some situations. Generally handles complex language well and understands detailed reasoning.
6	**Competent User**	Has generally effective command of the language despite some inaccuracies, inappropriacies and misunderstandings. Can use and understand fairly complex language, particularly in familiar situations.
5	**Modest User**	Has partial command of the language, coping with overall meaning in most situations, though is likely to make many mistakes. Should be able to handle basic communication in own field.
4	**Limited User**	Basic competence is limited to familiar situations. Has frequent problems in understanding and expression. Is not able to use complex language.
3	**Extremely Limited User**	Conveys and understands only general meaning in very familiar situations. Frequent breakdowns in communication occur.
2	**Intermittent User**	No real communication is possible except for the most basic information using isolated words or short formulae in familiar situations and to meet immediate needs. Has great difficulty understanding spoken and written English.
1	**Non User**	Essentially has no ability to use the language beyond possibly a few isolated words.
0	**Did Not Attempt The Test**	No assessable information provided

(Source: http://www.ielts.org/handbook.htm)

You will usually receive your results in around two weeks after taking the test. Results are valid for two years but different institutions may not accept your results as being current if you cannot prove ongoing English study. Check with the institution you are applying to study at.

- Your results will show a score for each section of the test as well as an overall score. You can get a half band score (4.5, 5.5, etc.) for Listening and Reading, but only full band scores (4, 5, 6, etc.) for the Writing and Speaking Sections.

- You cannot pass or fail this test – you are always given a score. Whether this score is high enough depends on what and where you want to study. Check with the institution at which you are applying to study.

You should also be honest with yourself about your English ability. Studying at university is hard enough in your native language, but to do so in a foreign language can be unbelievably hard. Most universities require a minimum overall score of 6.0 to enter an undergraduate course and 6.5 for postgraduate. This will, however, vary between courses and institutions, so check what your chosen institution needs.

Remember, if you don't get the required score in IELTS the first time, you have to wait another three months to retake the exam.

How can this book help?

1. It introduces you to the *different sections* of the IELTS Academic Module.
2. It familiarizes you with *the instructions, language and question-types* used in the IELTS tests.
3. It improves your English level by introducing you to *new language structures* and reinforcing what you already know.
4. It provides you with *four complete practice tests,* which should be taken under test conditions, and answers to those tests. A *Study Guide to the 404 Essential Tests for IELTS* is also available for you to contemplate the reasons why you got any answers wrong in these tests.

The information contained in this book has worked for many students who are now studying at universities in English-speaking countries.

If you are determined to succeed, you will need to:

1. read and practise the GENERAL POINTERS.
2. ensure that all practice tests are done under exam conditions.
3. familiarise yourself with the exam format.
4. immerse yourself in English as much as possible, particularly as you approach the exam date.

Some of the skills and language taught in different sections of this book will be referred to in other areas. For example, often the topics that are used in the reading and writing sections of the test are similar. Linking words (discourse markers) too, are not only useful in making a piece of writing more interesting – they can assist in finding an answer in the reading passages and help you to tune into an answer in the listening test.

What about the future?

The skills you learn in the 101…404 IELTS range can help you to achieve the academic standards necessary to perform well at university. The tips and hints that you adopt to ensure you get the required IELTS result should become part of your study skills repertoire at university. But remember – the required IELTS score is only the first step on the path to success at an English-speaking college or university. A good IELTS score is no guarantee that you will pass your course. It is, however, an indication that your English language level is of a sufficient standard to begin your chosen course – the rest is up to you.

TEST DESCRIPTION - LISTENING SECTION

You will be presented with four different listening passages with a variety of question types to answer.

LIMITS *Approximately 30 minutes*
Unlike the reading test, you will get extra time at the end to transfer your answers to the Answer Sheet.

There are FOUR distinct sections of 40 questions in total.
You will hear each section ONCE only.
Each listening is more difficult than the one preceding it.

Section 1	Section 2	Section 3	Section 4
Usually a conversation between two people. Sometimes a third person might be involved or introduced to the conversation. Usually in two parts. can be a social or an academic setting.	Usually a monologue of a social / functional nature. For example, an outing, a tour guide giving instructions or directions. Can be a social or academic setting.	Usually a conversation between two to four people. For example, a dialogue between two students regarding a tutorial, an assignement or oral presentation to be given. Usually in an academic setting.	Usually a lecture or speech given as a monologue. Sometimes the person is introduced by a second person at the beginning or a few questions might be asked during the course of the lecture. In an academic setting.
About 4 minutes listening time	About 3 - 4 minutes listening time	About 4 minutes listening time	At least 4 - 5 minutes listening time

A monologue = one person speaking
A dialogue (a conversation) = two or more people discussing a topic

The sections may be divided into two or more distinct parts. There may also be a pause in some of the sections to give you time to look at the questions relating to that part of the test.

It is important to note that poor spelling and incorrect grammar will be penalized, so you should check carefully after transferring your answers to the Answer Sheet.

POSSIBLE TOPIC AREAS:

Most of the IELTS listening tests are about social and educational situations. Often they are in an academic context set on a university campus discussing student orientation programs (introductions for new students to courses or institutions), details of assignments, classes or tutorials or plans for excursions, holidays or outings. The discussions might be between two students; a professor or lecturer and a student; or an administrator and a student.

The topics are usually of interest to students in their late teens or early twenties. There are information-giving and information-sharing situations.

As with the other sections of the IELTS test, you do not need to have any specialist knowledge to do well in the listening test.

GENERAL POINTERS:
- *Become familiar with the instructions used to introduce the sections.*
- *Read questions carefully and try to anticipate what you might hear.*
- *Use a highlighter pen to highlight key words.*
- *Think about and listen out for other forms of the key words and synonyms.*
- *Learn to identify question types.*
- *Know your numbers and figures!*
- *Keep looking forward to the next two questions, so you know where you are in the listening passage.*
- *Don't be distracted by anyone or anything – concentrate!*

GENERAL LISTENING ADVICE

Do	Don't
Read the questions before the start of each section and highlight key words.	Don't panic if you miss an answer.
Listen out for linking words and discourse markers to help you follow what is happening.	Don't guess any answers unless you cannot find the answer or evidence for an answer and your time is almost up.
Check your spelling and grammar. Does the word you have chosen fit grammatically, and should it be singular or plural?	Don't listen for enjoyment - your purpose is to answer the questions only.
Look for synonyms of key words in questions. Guess - if you cannot find the answer.	Don't worry if you can't understand or hear every word. Remember that the rhythm of spoken English means that the most important words are always stressed the most. Learn to listen for those.
Transfer answers quickly but carefully.	Don't leave any spaces on your answer sheet - you don't lose marks for wrong answers.

WORDS / TOPICS / PHRASES OFTEN USED IN LISTENING QUESTIONS:

The words and topics listed here are not restricted to particular sections of the listening test.

Section 1	Section 2	Section 3	Section 4
personal details	information giving	information sharing	information giving
number sequences	money, prices	drafts	lecture
phone and fax numbers	dates	plagiarism	I'd like to begin with
addresses	giving directions	seminar	...which leads me to...
postcodes	maps	tutorials	in other words
dates	before that	tutor	What I mean by that is
opening and closing times	plus	lecture	To sum up
family name	refundable deposit	lecturer	study guide
first name	non-refundable	textbooks	orientation
4 in the morning till 6 tonight	altogether	resource	series of lectures
decimal pont	includes the $4 each way single (ticket)	research	due to
percentage %	£10 return (trip)	extension	outline
Celsius °C	cents	due date	
Fahrenheit °F	pence		
degrees	the high street		
double 6 (66)	the main street in the town		
triple 7 (777)	for up to two weeks		
fractions ¼ ½			
registration			
student number			

QUESTION TYPES:

The IELTS listening tests use a variety of question types which are described in the table below.

Type of question	Example of direction given on tape	Skills needed	Test strategies
Multiple choice	*In Questions 1 - 5, circle the correct answer.*	Identifying types of answers expected - what, why, when, etc. Listening for specific information.	Highlight key words in questions. Identify answers that seem unlikely & then find proof before eliminating them.
Short-answer questions	*Answer Questions 1 - 5.*	Listening for specific information. Identifying parts of speech used and required.	Highlight key words. Listen for specific words but also ideas - paraphrase.
Completing sentences, tables, flow-charts, forms, summaries, etc.	*Complete Questions 1 - 5 by using* **NO MORE THAN THREE WORDS.** *Complete the following table according to...* *Fill in the gaps...* *Mark on the map...*	Distinguishing between examples and main ideas. Identifying parts of speech. Identifying discourse markers and signposting (words that show you what part the speaker is on - e.g. First, next, then etc.) Identifying headings and main ideas.	Contractions are not used when word-limits are given. Don't use more than the number of words allotted. Look at given information to identify the type of information required. Scan given notes in summaries to frame your own note-taking.
Labelling diagrams	*Listen to the directions and choose the appropriate letter.* *Label the diagram by writing...*	Understanding relationships between words (discourse markers). Sequencing and following chronological order. Listening for specific information.	Brainstorm any vocabulary or knowledge that you have of the picture or topic.
Classifying	*Study the table and place the articles in the correct column.* *Write A for Always, N for Never and R for Rarely.*	Understanding the relationship between words. Listening for specific information. Distinguishing examples from main ideas.	Use a highlighter to separate different characteristics of categories. Use given information to determine relationships if necessary.
Matching lists, phrases or pictures	*Choose the picture which best shows...* *Match the places with the...*	Listening for specific information. Understanding cause and effect.	Identify the most obvious answers but then find proof before selecting them.

IMMERSION IDEAS:

1. Make sure you know how words sound – say unfamiliar words aloud, don't just read them silently.

2. Listen to as much English as possible – listen to different accents including British English on the BBC, Australian English on the ABC and American English on Voice of America, watch DVDs in English.

3. Use some of the following websites to listen to English:

   www.bbc.co.uk/worldservice/index.shtml;
   www.esl-lab.com; www.cnn.com; www.abc.net.au.

TEST DESCRIPTION - READING SECTION

You will be presented with three different *passages* with a variety of question types to answer. The texts are similar to those you would find in journals, textbooks and magazines. If technical words are used, a glossary will be provided to explain their meanings.

LIMITS *60 minutes including transfer of answers to a separate Answer Sheet*

There are three passages of 40 questions in total.
Each passage will contain between 750 to 900 words.
Each passage is more difficult than the one preceding it.
The different question types within each passage get progressively more difficult.

It is difficult to predict the content of the reading passages in the IELTS test but the topics covered in the reading section are often similar to the topics in the writing section. Remember that the IELTS test does not require you to have any specialist knowledge prior to taking the test and that the answers will therefore be in the texts themselves – you just need to find them!

POSSIBLE TOPIC AREAS:

There are too many to mention – see topics in the writing section. Also, expect some scientific or complex subject matter as diverse as mining processes and the effects of radiation or logging rainforests to industrial and work-related issues, conservation issues or transport.

WORDS / PHRASES OFTEN USED IN READING QUESTIONS:

Before taking the test, you should be familiar with all of the following words or phrases –

> according to the information
> appropriate
> classify
> consequences
> contradict
> correlation
> correspond
> factors
> flow chart
> glossary
> headings
> illustrated by the diagram
> label
> mentioned
> summary or summarise
> theme

GENERAL POINTERS:
- *Never read any text before looking at the related questions.*
- *Use titles, headings, underlined or highlighted words and diagrams as part of your scanning process.*
- *Read the first and last sentences in each paragraph to locate topic sentences.*
- *Learn to identify question types.*
- *Think about synonyms, paraphrases and modal verbs.*
- *Remember the time-limit – 15 minutes per text should be your goal.*
- *Buy a highlighter pen and use it!*

GENERAL READING ADVICE

Do	Don't
Read the questions before reading the passage.	Don't start reading without knowing why you are reading.
Check if there is a glossary - use diagrams, highlighted words, titles and headings to help you get a general idea of the text.	Don't guess any answers unless you cannot find the answer or evidence for an answer and your time is almost up.
Be conscious of discourse markers to establish relationships between words, sentences and paragraphs.	Don't read for enjoyment - your purpose is to answer the questions only.
Use context clues and word-building skills to understand difficult words.	Don't deviate from your exam time plan..
Look for synonyms in the reading passage of key words in questions.	Don't worry about unknown words unless they are necessary.
Guess - if you cannot find the answer.	Don't leave any spaces on your Answer Sheet - you don't lose marks for wrong answers.
Think about which type of answers can be guessed very quickly if you are short of time (True/False and multiple choice, for example).	
Transfer answers quickly but carefully.	

SUGGESTED EXAM TIMEPLAN FOR READING SECTION:

You have 60 minutes to complete the reading section of the IELTS test. You must transfer your answers to the answer sheet provided WITHIN THAT TIME.

0:00	Begin Passage 1 – start by glancing at the title, diagrams, pictures, headings, etc. Then, read the questions and answer as many as possible.
0:15	Guess remainder of questions that relate to Passage 1, but put a question-mark beside these to remind yourself later that you have guessed these answers.
0:16	Begin Passage 2 – read the questions and answer as many as possible.
0:31	Guess remainder of questions that relate to Passage 2 but again, put a question-mark beside these to remind yourself later.
0:32	Begin Passage 3 – read the questions and answer as many as possible.
0:50	Guess remainder of questions that relate to Passage 3.
0:51	Go back to Passage 1 – try answering the guessed questions.
0:53	Go back to Passage 2 – try answering the guessed questions.
0:55	Transfer all questions carefully but quickly to the answer sheet.
0:58	Use the remaining time to double-check any answers to the last few questions in Reading Passage 3 that you guessed earlier.

Remember that each passage is more difficult than the preceding one.

Allow 15 minutes each for Passages 1 and 2 but give yourself 18 minutes to complete Passage 3.

Remember however, that you will have time to go back and check on your guesses at the end of the test – do not spend time checking your answers or changing your answers.

Practise all tests using this formula.

QUESTION TYPES:

A variety of question types is used in the reading passages and you need to be familiar with techniques used in each. If any other question type is used, the test will include an example – however, this is unusual.

Type of question	Example of direction used	Skills needed	Test strategies
Multiple choice	*Choose the correct letter(s)* OR *Choose the correct letters for each answer ...and write them in boxes 1 - 5 on your Answer Sheet.*	Skimming for general impression or gist. Scanning for specific (usually factual) information. Understanding the relationships between words and paragraphs (discourse markers).	Highlight key words. Eliminate other answers.
Short-answer questions	*Answer the following questions with **NO MORE THAN THREE WORDS** which must be taken from the text. Write your answers in boxes 6 - 10 on your Answer Sheet.*	Scanning for specific information.	Use techniques to find answers to *who, what, when, where* questions. Highlight key words in questions and look for these key words or synonyms in the passage.
Choosing from a heading bank	*From the list of headings below choose the most suitable heading for Sections 1 - 9 in Reading Passage 4. Then, write your answers in boxes 11 - 15 on your Answer Sheet.*	Skimming for general impression or gist. Identifying main ideas in paragraphs. Locating topic sentences.	Always read headings first and then topic sentences (or first sentence in paragraphs). Do not read whole paragraph. Do not complete in order given. Choose most obvious answer first. Roman numerals are often used: I, II, III, IV, V etc.
Matching lists and phrases	*By referring to Passage 2, match the list of phrases A - E with Steps 1 - 6. Write the correct letters in boxes 31 - 36 on your Answer Sheet.*	Understanding relationships between words and paragraphs (discourse markers). Paraphrasing and synonyms.	Choose the most obvious answers first.

Table continues on the next page...

QUESTION TYPES continued:

Type of question	Example of direction used	Skills needed	Test strategies
Identifying viewpoints, facts and opinions	*Look at the following statements and indicate TRUE if the statement agrees with the information in the passage, FALSE if the statement does not agree, and NOT GIVEN if there is insufficient information in the passage.* *Do the following statements agree with (reflect) the views of the writer in Passage 3? Write YES, NO, or NOT GIVEN in boxes 21 - 25 on your Answer Sheet.*	Recognising opinions and viewpoints. Recognising main ideas. Interpreting information. Making inferences.	Look at the language used in the passage - is it negative or positive when discussing the topic? Is it emotional or factual / technical? Be careful of questions that use broad statements like *all, always.* Make sure that you know the differences in meanings of modal verbs.
Classifying	*Using information provided in Passage 2, classify the following animals as Category A, B, or C. Write your answers in boxes 26 - 30 on your Answer Sheet.*	Scanning for information. Understanding relationships between words and passages (discourse markers). Paraphrasing and synonyms.	Use a highlighter to identify the character of different categories in the text.
Completing sentences, tables, flow charts, summaries, etc.	*Use **NO MORE THAN THREE WORDS** to complete the sentence* OR *Choose from the list of words given below to complete the summary.* *Then, write your answers in boxes 11 - 15 on your Answer Sheet.*	Scanning for information. Summarising. Identifying parts of speech. Paraphrasing. Sequencing.	Contractions are not used when word limits are given. Don't use more than the number of words allotted. Check the question to see if it asks for your own words or words from the text. For summaries and clozes, make sure that you have a general understanding of the passage before starting to complete. Information in summaries and clozes is usually in the same order as the passage.

IMMERSION IDEAS:

1. Read as much English as possible – buy magazines such as "National Geographic", "Newsweek" and "Time"; become aware of current social issues and discuss them in English with your friends.

2. Buy English newspapers.

3. Borrow a couple of English science textbooks and try following some process descriptions. This will also help your Task 1 writing.

4. Use some of the following websites to see what's current:

   www.ap.com; www.reuters.com; www.news.com.au; www.cnn.com; www.bbc.co.uk.

TEST DESCRIPTION - WRITING SECTION

The writing section of the IELTS test Academic Module consists of two tasks – both requiring different skills.

Task 1: Reporting on a given table, graph, chart, etc or describing a process, procedure and / or how something works. In some questions you will be required to compare two (or more) given sources of statistical-type information or data.

> **LIMITS** *20 minutes (recommended only)*
> *Minimum 150 words (no maximum limit)*

Task 2: Expressing your own opinion or an argument for and/or against a particular topic. In some questions, you may be required to put forward possible solutions or analyse problems regarding certain topics. You will be required to write one of five different types of academic essays.

> **LIMITS** *40 minutes (recommended only)*
> *Minimum 250 words (no maximum limit)*

POSSIBLE TOPIC AREAS & QUESTION TYPES:

Task 1:

You should expect to see statistical information or data represented in tables, graphs or diagrams. You will be asked to write a short description (150 words minimum) based on these representations. As such, Task 1 will give you all the information that you will need to complete the essay.

Remember that it is not really the topic that is important in this question, rather you will be judged on your ability to interpret the information from statistics.

You should expect to see the following kinds of subjects – this list is not definitive:

> population trends
> immigration patterns
> leisure and sporting activities
> injuries or deaths
> education choices
> food – fast food, diet, obesity
> weather patterns including rainfall or lack of it
> economic-type statistics including cost of living, life expectancy, etc.

Sometimes Task 1 requires you to describe how something works or to describe a process. For this kind of task you should expect to see the following kinds of topics:

> manufacturing or sorting processes
> organisational charts
> food chains
> life cycles, etc.

Task 2:

You should expect to see tasks based on social, environmental and economic issues and concerns. The following list contains topics that anyone entering university, at either a graduate or postgraduate level, would be able to discuss or have either an interest in or an opinion about:

ENVIRONMENTAL TOPICS such as:

> logging rainforests
> pollution
> the ozone layer
> the Greenhouse Effect
> whaling, excess packaging
> extinction of a species

SOCIAL TOPICS such as:

social welfare
unemployment
effects of tourism on culture
globalisation
vegetarianism
standards for safety in a variety of settings
the impact or effects of technology on society

ECONOMICS TOPICS such as:

the development of third world countries
developed countries giving aid to developing countries
use of non-renewable resources to keep countries' economies viable

You will also be asked to produce a certain style of writing to suit the task in question, which may include any of the following:

- Argument
- Cause and Effect
- Comparison and Contrast
- Advantages and Disadvantages (discursive)
- Report

NOTE: the writing section is scored in full band scores, not half band scores. That is, you cannot get a score of 6.5 in the writing, it will either be a 6 or 7.

WORDS OFTEN USED IN WRITING TASK 1 AND TASK 2 QUESTIONS:

to what extent	evaluate
to what degree	analyse
how far	consider
what level of	make recommendations
describe	explain
discuss	write a report
write an argument	write a case for

ASSESSMENT:

Knowing how your writing is assessed should help you to improve your writing skills for the IELTS test.

Skills tested in both Tasks 1 and 2

- Spelling and punctuation should be of a standard that does not negatively interfere with the understanding of the essay.
- The register, style and content should be appropriate and relevant for the task.
- Grammar and sentence structure should show variety and maturity.
- The question should be analysed and answered correctly – the task has to be fulfilled.

Additional skills tested in Task 1:

The following will be tested – the student's ability to

- present information in a well-organised, easy-to-follow way.
- compare and contrast information.
- compare and contrast opposing arguments.
- describe an illustrated process or procedure.
- explain how something operates.
- identify relationships or trends in data.

Additional skills tested in Task 2:

The following will be tested – the student's ability to

- present opinions in a logical, clear way.
- justify an opinion and exemplify appropriately.
- present both sides of an argument.
- evaluate both sides of an argument.
- compare and contrast opposing arguments

Candidates are advised to ask themselves these questions after completing the tasks.

Task 1 -

Is the information presented in a well-organised way which makes it easy to read and follow?
Is the information compared and contrasted?
Are relationships and trends identified?
Is the process or procedure described clearly and systematically?

Does the spelling and punctuation hinder understanding of the essay?
Is the register, style and content appropriate for the task?
Does the grammar and sentence structure used show variety and maturity?
Has the task been fulfilled – did the student answer the question and complete the task?
Is the length of the answer at least 150 words?

Task 2 -

Are opinions presented in a logical, clear way?
Are opinions justified and exemplified appropriately?
Were both sides of the argument presented?
Were both sides of the argument evaluated?

Does the spelling and punctuation hinder understanding of the essay?
Is the register, style and content appropriate for the task?
Does the grammar and sentence structure used show variety and maturity?
Has the task been fulfilled – did the student answer the question and complete the task?
Have you written at least 250 words?

GENERAL POINTERS:
- *Learn to interpret questions and identify question types and writing styles.*
- *Practise and rewrite corrected essays.*
- *Decide which task you will do first and make this decision long before the test date.*
- *It is important to understand that your writing cannot improve without much practice.*

GENERAL WRITING ADVICE

Do	Don't
Be mindful of the time limits.	Don't use a dictionary when you practise your writing, as you can't take one into the exam.
Read the question carefully and then check that you have answered the question correctly.	Don't try to analyse the tables in Task 1, just describe the information.
Take time to plan the things you are going to write. You need arguments and examples to support your ideas.	Don't spend too long on Task 1. You need to allocate about 20 minutes to that. After that time, go on to Task 2.
Think about using linking and sequencing words to help your writing to sound more cohesive.	Don't use the same vocabulary all the time.
Learn different ways of describing graphs and tables.	Don't use the same sentence structure and linking words. Show your knowledge by using variety and complexity.
Make sure in Task 2 that you have time to write a conclusion. Your answer will be incomplete without one.	

The two writing tasks in the IELTS test are different in many ways and as such should be prepared for and practised differently. The *Study Guide for 404 Essential Tests for IELTS* looks at the steps involved in the writing process for both tasks using concrete examples and sample answers. It includes guidelines that IELTS candidates can use to frame answers in suitable structures.

IMMERSION IDEAS:

1. Do at least one piece of writing per week in examination-mode – start immediately and use the practice exercises given in 202 *Useful Exercises for IELTS*.

   Always be mindful of the time limits.

   Don't use a dictionary as you practise your writing – you can't use one in the test.

2. Become knowledgeable about the probable topics you will be asked to write about – particularly in Task 2.

   Discuss them in English with friends and build your vocabulary regarding these topics.

3. Familiarise yourself with different sentence structures; the passive voice and words (in particular, verbs and adverbs) that will aid you in completing the task.

4. For Task 1, find websites that give you statistical information, and try to interpret that information.

   www.forbes.com; www.morganbanks.com; www.un.org

TEST DESCRIPTION - SPEAKING SECTION

Many students find this part of the IELTS test the most daunting because it happens face-to-face with the examiner – there is no hiding. However, it shouldn't be an unpleasant experience and there are many opportunities to help yourself. For instance, you should be aware that you can ask for a question to be repeated. The interview is the shortest of the four tests and most candidates cannot believe how quickly the time goes. The one thing that you have to remember is that it is a speaking test – if you don't speak and make a deliberate attempt to show the examiner your ability, then the examiner has no choice but to give you a low mark. Most examiners want to give you a good score, but they will not do so, unless you communicate effectively with them.

LIMITS *Total interview time is from 11 - 14 minutes*
3 parts in total

Part 1	Part 2	Part 3
Introduction & interview	Long turn	Two-way discussion between you and the examiner
The examiner wants to get to know who you are and what you like doing. He / she will also try to relax you so that you don't feel too nervous.	The examiner will give you a card with details of a particular topic. He / she will give you about a minute to prepare for your long turn to speak.	The examiner will ask you more difficult questions related to the topic in Part 2. The questions are designed to test your speaking level. Answer the questions as best you can.
Relax - answer the questions in full sentences.	Take your time and speak clearly and sensibly.	
About 4 - 5 minutes	About 3 - 4 minutes which includes preparation time	About 4 - 5 minutes

POSSIBLE TOPIC AREAS:

Part 1 topics are usually general in nature – asking about you, your family, your interests, what you do, your study and what your future plans are. It is an introduction, so consider the type of things that an English-speaking person might ask when they first meet you. Speak clearly.

Part 2 topics might focus on such topics as:

- a particular person such as a teacher you had in school, a famous person or a sporting celebrity,
- a particular event like the Olympics or the start of the millennium,
- a place that you have visited etc.

There are prompts on the card to help you structure your long turn, so make sure that you use these prompts wisely. Don't ignore them.

Part 3 is designed to test your speaking ability. The examiner will ask you questions that give you the opportunity to exhibit your range of vocabulary and grammatical structures. Answer the questions as fully as possible and if you don't understand a question, ask for it to be repeated.

NOTE: the speaking section is scored in full band scores, not half band scores. That is, you cannot get a score of 6.5 in the speaking. It will either be a 6 or 7.

QUESTION TYPES:

It is impossible to tell you the precise questions that will be asked in the Speaking Test but if you consider the type of speech functions that are being tested, you can prepare yourself more adequately.

In the IELTS speaking interview, you should be prepared to

- give information (personal and non-personal)
- give your opinion and justify it
- explain and/or suggest something
- express your preference for something
- compare and/or contrast something
- summarise and analyse
- describe something or narrate an event
- speculate
- check on comprehension
- repair, maintain and extend a conversation.

Impressing the examiner and increasing your band score:

It is possible to achieve an IELTS band score of 5 or above, if you have an intermediate level of English. (5 is often the minimum required for speaking for entry to any tertiary program.) A candidate who achieves Band 5 is described as a Modest User "... coping with overall meaning in most situations", still "... likely to make many mistakes" but "... able to handle basic communication in own field."

Before undertaking an IELTS test, ask yourself if you can

- communicate effectively in English with your peers.
- use some complex grammatical structures accurately e.g. all basic tenses, all conditionals (except perhaps 3rd conditional), the passive voice.
- insert discourse markers and linking words into your conversation.
- manage to express most ideas without having to get new vocabulary from the dictionary.
- make complex sentences that explain and extend your ideas.
- understand a variety of English accents (e.g. British, Australian, American, New Zealand, Canadian)
- use appropriate conversational and cultural interaction in a variety of situations.

Answering yes to all of these points, means that you have the ability to score a minimum 5 in IELTS, if your performance in each of the three parts of the interview demonstrates this ability.

In order to improve your result, you must demonstrate the ability to carry out all of the speech functions listed above, without making systematic technical errors – that is, grammar, vocabulary or (sentence) structure errors that occur repeatedly. Systematic errors can be identified by practising for the speaking interview, recording yourself, listening critically and evaluating yourself or getting your teacher to evaluate your performance. If you are making the same type of error, remedy the problem by doing some appropriate exercises.

Do not take the IELTS test if you are making lots of systematic errors. Systematic misuse of prepositions, subject/verb agreement, plurals, articles and word order will alert the examiner to your specific language problems.

Finally, remember that you do not have to speak perfect English to achieve a band score of between 5 and above. However, you do need to impress the examiner. A positive, confident attitude will help.

GENERAL POINTERS:
- *Learn to speak clearly using appropriate vocabulary.*
- *Practise using different sentence structures.*
- *Practise paraphrasing – if you don't know a particular word, try to explain what you mean using different words.*
- *Get some strategies to repair the conversation if things go wrong*
- *If you can't think of a real situation to talk about, imagine one; the examiner doesn't know or care if you are telling the truth, just that you are speaking.*
- *It is important to understand that your speaking cannot improve without much practice.*

GENERAL SPEAKING ADVICE

Do	Don't
Speak clearly and answer in full sentences.	Don't speak too softly.
Look at the examiner and maintain eye contact when possible.	Don't give yes or no answers.
Ask for something to be repeated if you do not understand what you are expected to do.	Don't try to be somebody else - just relax and answer the questions as well as you can.
Take the time to plan for Part 2.	Don't worry about speaking too much - the examiner will control the timing of your responses.
Vary the words and phrases you use.	Don't try to give a rehearsed speech.
Be well-mannered and respectful throughout the interview.	Don't stop trying throughout the interview.

IMMERSION IDEAS:

1. Become comfortable speaking in English – that means speaking in English as often as possible. Find friends or colleagues who will speak to you in English.

2. Practise the different parts of the interview with different people. Build your vocabulary and discuss different topics.

3. Familiarise yourself with different grammatical structures – practise using difficult structures like conditionals and standard introductory phrases like:

   "Well, in my opinion…".

4. Record yourself taking the practice test interviews and critically listen to yourself. If possible, ask a teacher or native-speaker to give you feedback on your performance. Focus on any systematic errors that appear.

5. Read about the speaking module in *101 Helpful Hints for IELTS* and use the prepared questions to practise your interview style.

HOW TO TAKE THE PRACTICE TESTS

Before Taking the Practice Tests

- Read the Listening, Reading, Writing and Speaking Test Descriptions provided in this book.
- Read and practise the General Pointers included in the Test Descriptions.
- Familiarise yourself with the question types, specialised vocabulary and test format – all provided in this book.

- Find a quiet room.
- Allow three hours to complete each test.
- Ensure that you are not going to be interrupted.
- Take a highlighter pen, a pen or pencil and blank copies of a Listening Test Answer Sheet and a Reading Test Answer Sheet.
- Take paper to complete the writing tasks – IELTS will provide a special page for this, on the day of the actual test.
- Take a cassette player for the Listening Test and a blank tape to use for the Speaking Interview.
- Take a clock or a watch.

During a Practice Test

- Strictly follow the timings for all parts of the IELTS test – that means doing the practice test under exam conditions.
- Complete the test in the same order as they appear – Listening, Reading, Writing and then the Speaking Interview.
- Allow yourself 10 minutes to transfer your Listening Test answers onto the Answer Sheet.

After Taking Practice Test 1

- Check your answers to the Listening and Reading Tests with those provided in the Answer Keys section of this book.
- Model Answers and extensive discussion of all the writing tasks is provided in the *Study Guide to the 404 Essential Tests for IELTS*.
- Critically listen to the tape-recording of your answers to the Speaking Interview questions and answer the questions provided in the Answer Keys section.
- Use the Score Analyser as a guide to determine your possible IELTS band score for each of the tests.

After Taking Practice Tests 1, 2 and 3

- Carry out the steps as outlined for Practice Test 1.
- Use the Score Analyser as a guide to determine if your errors are systematic.
- Focus on the errors that you are making – use the *Study Guide to the 404 Essential Tests* in conjunction with these tests; re-read appropriate sections from *101 Helpful Hints for IELTS* or *202 Useful Exercises for IELTS*.

After Taking Practice Test 4

- Carry out all of the above steps.
- Use the Score Analyser once again to determine your possible IELTS band score for each of the tests.
- Enrol for your IELTS test.

A motivated student, immersed in English and taking full-time intensive English classes, with support from an experienced teacher, should be able to improve by one full band scale in a ten to twelve week period.

PRACTICE TEST 1 - LISTENING

SECTION 1: QUESTIONS 1 – 10

Listen to two students, Louise and Kerry, talking about their vacation.

Questions 1 – 4

Answer the questions below.
*Use **NO MORE THAN THREE WORDS OR A NUMBER** for each answer.*

Example:	Where did Louise spend her summer holidays?	.......................**Europe**........................

1 How much was a Eurailpass Youth Ticket? ....

2 How many European countries did Louise's ticket allow her to travel to? ....

....

3 Did the Eurailpass Youth Ticket include the train from London to Paris? ....

....

4 How old must you be if you want to purchase a Eurailpass Youth ticket? ....

....

Questions 5 – 10

Complete the notes below.
*Use **NO MORE THAN THREE WORDS** for each answer.*

Points that Louise makes about Eurail:

- easy to travel to small towns
- easy to meet (5) ....
- (6) .... with times of the trains
- night-trains had many (7) .... as passengers

Advice that Louise gives about Eurail:

- Don't take (8) .... bags
- Be (9) .... with your belongings
- Spend enough time in each country to experience (10) ....

SECTION 2: QUESTIONS 11 – 20

Questions 11 - 16

Complete the table below.
*Use **NO MORE THAN THREE WORDS** for each answer.*

Central City University - Student Support Services		
Academic Support Services	Course Content & Assessment Advisors	- counselling re: course selection
	(11)	- language support
Library Services	Research & Resource Department	- assistance and advice for research and library use
	Study Skills Department	- assistance with arranging (12) ....
	(13)	- arrange computer logon and password
Administration Student Services	Administration Officers	- issuing student cards
	(14)	- independent accommodation advice
	Homestay Officer	- family-style accommodation advice
	Student Employment Officer	- part-time and vacation employment
	(15)	- inquiries re: passports and visas
	Bookshop	- retail outlet
Student Union Services	Student Counselling Service	- counselling re: (16) .... problems
	Equal Opportunity Services	- petitioning and sexual harassment
	Activity & Clubs Services	- availability of clubs and activity schedules

Questions 17 - 20

Match the names of the buildings with the letters on the map below.

17 The Library .... 19 Bookshop ....

18 Administration Building .... 20 International Student Advisor ....

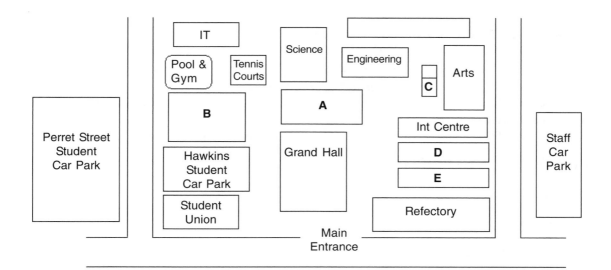

SECTION 3: QUESTIONS 21 – 30

Questions 21 – 22

*Choose the correct letter from **A - C**.*

21 Rose's plan for the tutorial is to research and present
    A the differences between male and female children.
    B the different ways that male and female children are raised.
    C the differences between male and female parenting.

22 The British experiments that Rose refers to in the conversation
    A were carried out in 100 families.
    B observed girls and boys who were raised identically.
    C noted the different treatments male and females received.

Questions 23 - 26

*Choose **TWO** letters from **A - E** for each answer.*

23 & 24 This tutorial will
    A require Marie and Rose to carry out research.
    B interest the tutor and their classmates.
    C be tested.
    D help Marie to catch up on her research work.
    E benefit other assessment that Rose and Marie have to do.

25 & 26   Before starting their preparation, Marie and Rose must

      A   catch up on other work.
      B   agree on the topic.
      C   get approval from the tutor.
      D   make an appointment to see a librarian.
      E   plan carefully for the next two weeks.

Questions 27 - 30

Complete the form below.
*Use **NO MORE THAN THREE WORDS** for each answer.*

Proposed Tutorial Topics	
Tutor: *Jim Clark* Department: **(27)**	Subject Code: *EC 101*
Topic: *'How The Sexes Differ'* Aims of tutorial: 1. *To show* **(28)** .... 2. *To show the differences are* (29) .... Day & Date of tutorial: *Tuesday 26th*	Time: *11 a.m.* Room: *B 1203*

A/V Equipment request
 	
   ☐   TV   ☐   Tape recorder
   ☐ Video ☑ Overhead Projector	

(30) How do you want to be notified of lecturer's approval?
 	
   ☐   PHONE   ☐   LETTER
   ☐ FAX ☐ IN PERSON	

SECTION 4:   QUESTIONS 31 – 40

Questions 31 – 32

Complete the following sentences.
*Use **NO MORE THAN THREE WORDS** for each answer:*

31   The speaker identifies the following two differences between being a high school student and a university student:

- the academic expectations of tutors and lecturers are ....

- students must take responsibility for their own learning.

32   The speaker aims to get students to recognise exam stress and the way it can affect

....

Questions 33 - 36

Complete the table below.
Use **NO MORE THAN THREE WORDS** *for each answer.*

EXAM STRESS	
Signs	**Effective Management includes:**
Physiological: Increased pulse-rate Perspiration Breathing problems Problems with **(33)**	**(34)** .... breathing exercises
Psychological: Irrational **(35)** .... Panic	Be confident and **(36)** .... Be calm and analyse the questions

Questions 37 - 40

Complete the following notes.
Use **NO MORE THAN THREE WORDS** *for each answer.*

37   Time needed to study effectively will .... according to individuals.

38   Time Management involves taking notice of the allocation of .... to exam
     questions.

39   To achieve good grades in examinations at university, you need to:

     • have academic ability.

     • be ....

     • think clearly.

     • observe time management practices.

40   Students wishing to develop their .... can attend next week's workshop.

PRACTICE TEST 1 - READING

READING PASSAGE 1

Questions 1 - 13 are based on Reading Passage 1.

THE LIFE CYCLE OF A STAR

It has been conservatively estimated that there are some 10,000 billion, billion stars in the universe. It is difficult to know the exact age of a star (astronomers have identified stars as young as 25,000 years old and others are thought to be over 10 billion years old), but what astronomers do know is that there are many different kinds. How each star is formed, and its mass, influences its type and longevity.

A star is born in a nebula, which is a giant cloud of gas and dust. The larger the amount of matter that is in the nebula, the greater the mass of the star that is created. Inside these nebulae are dense areas of gas, which, due to their density, have a stronger gravitational pull than the rest of the nebula. Gradually, gravity drags the gas in the nebula together and it begins to spin and become increasingly hotter. Once the temperature reaches 15,000,000°C, nuclear fusion occurs in the centre of the cloud, and it begins to glow brightly. It stabilizes at this temperature, contracts slightly and becomes what is known as a main sequence star (an example of this is our own Sun). It can remain in this stage for millions or billions of years.

As it glows, hydrogen in the centre (through the nuclear fusion) becomes helium. Eventually the hydrogen supply in the core diminishes and the core of the star becomes unstable, contracting more. However, the outer parts of the star (which are still mainly hydrogen) expand and cool, and in doing so, the star starts to glow red. It is at this stage that the star becomes a red giant. It is anticipated that it will take the Sun another 5 billion years to reach this stage. By then it will have grown large enough to engulf the three closest planets (Mercury, Venus and Earth) and glow 2,000 times brighter than it currently does.

Exactly how a star will react in the red giant phase depends on its mass. Throughout the red giant phase, the hydrogen in the outer parts carries on burning, and the centre gets hotter and hotter. On reaching 200,000,000°C, the helium atoms fuse forming carbon atoms. The remainder of the hydrogen explodes and forms a ring around the core called a planetary nebula.

With medium-sized stars, once the final helium atoms have fused into carbon atoms, the star starts to die. The gravitational pull leads to the last of the star's matter collapsing inwards and compacting to become extremely dense. A star like this is called a white dwarf. It will shine white-hot until the remaining energy (thermal energy trapped in its interior) has been exhausted after which it will no longer emit light. This can take in excess of several billion years. It is then termed a black dwarf (a cold, dark star, perhaps replete with diamonds) and remains in that stage forever.

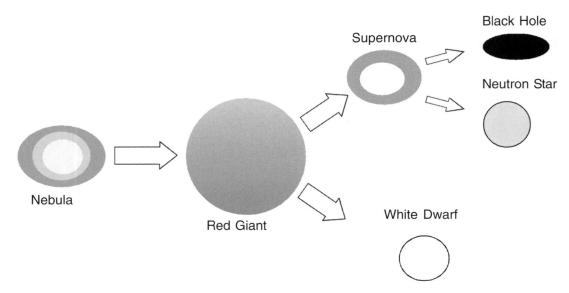

Nebula → Red Giant → Supernova → Black Hole / Neutron Star

White Dwarf

When the larger red giants (massive stars) collapse, which happens in an instant, so much planetary nebula is created that this gas and dust can be used as building material for planets in developing solar systems.   In addition, with massive stars, as the temperature increases, the carbon atoms get pulled together to form increasingly heavier elements like oxygen, nitrogen and finally iron. Once this happens, fusion ceases and the iron atoms begin absorbing energy. At some point in the future, this energy is released in a huge explosion called a supernova. A supernova can have a core temperature of up to 1,000,000,000°C and the explosion can light up the sky for weeks, outshining an entire galaxy. Astronomers believe that Earth is made up of elements formed from the inside of stars, in particular red giants that exploded as supernovas. These massive stars have an average life span of one million years.

After becoming a supernova, the remaining core of a massive star that is 1.5 to 4 times as massive as the Sun becomes a neutron star. It starts to spin and often emits radio waves. If these waves occur in pulses, the neutron star is referred to as a pulsar. When a massive star has eight or more times the mass of the Sun, it will remain massive after the supernova. It has no nuclear fusion supporting the core and becomes engulfed by its own gravity. This results in a black hole, which sucks in any matter or energy that passes close to it. The gravitational field of a black hole is powerful enough to prevent the escape of light and is so dense that it cannot be measured. The phrase 'black hole' originated from the physicist John Archibald Wheeler; before this, black holes were known as 'frozen stars.' Wheeler came up with this name two years before the proof of the existence of the first black hole, X-ray binary star Cygnus X-1, in 1971. Astronomers think that there may be a black hole at the centre of each galaxy.

The life cycle of a star is really that – the materials from an exploded star mix with the hydrogen of the universe. This mixture in turn will be the starting point of the next star. The Sun is a case in point, containing the debris from numerous other stars that exploded long before the Sun was born.

Questions 1 - 6

*Different stages and types of stars are mentioned in Reading Passage 1. Choose **ONE** of the types or stages (**A - H**) from the box below which best matches the descriptions (**Questions 1 – 6**). Write your answers in boxes 1 - 6 on your Answer Sheet.*

NOTE: *you may use any answer more than once.*

A	nebula	**E**	black dwarf
B	main sequence star	**F**	supernova
C	red giant	**G**	neutron star
D	white dwarf	**H**	black hole

		Answer
Example:	hottest, brightest point of a star	**F**
1	the Sun	B
2	birthplace of a star	....
3	a dying star	....
4	sometimes has pulsating waves	....
5	its size is immeasurable	....
6	its supply of energy has run out	....

Questions 7 - 13

Complete the sentences using **NO MORE THAN THREE** *words for each answer. Write your answers in boxes 7 - 13 on your Answer Sheet.*

7   Hydrogen will turn to helium after .... occurs.

8   The colour of the red giant is formed as the .... becomes smaller and the outer areas cool.

9   At 200,000,000°C the star's helium atoms fuse into carbon atoms, and then the star

    ....

10 Unlike small and medium-sized stars, large stars .... quickly.

11 A black hole's .... stops light from being emitted.

12 Astronomers knew about .... before they were able to confirm their existence.

13 Planets and stars are likely to consist of .... from exploded celestial bodies.

READING PASSAGE 2

Questions 14 - 27 are based on Reading Passage 2.

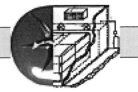

TOMATO RIPENING

Tomatoes give off minute quantities of ethylene gas which is active in starting the natural ripening process. If left to nature; however, the tomatoes ripen in a random way. The trickled ethylene gas process of tomato ripening consists of exposing the tomatoes to a low concentration of ethylene gas under controlled temperature conditions in a special tomato-ripening room. This treatment initiates and controls the speed of the natural ripening and colouring process in the tomatoes.

Controlled ripening and colouring enables the grower to market tomatoes of more uniform colour and quality than is possible with green or field-ripened produce. Timing of harvesting and marketing may, within limits, also be regulated by the use of controlled ripening and colouring in order to achieve maximum returns and make the best use of labour and equipment.

Ripening Conditions

All fruit must be mature green at harvest for controlled ripening to be successfully carried out. Relative humidity does not appear to be of great importance in the tomato-ripening process. Little moisture loss from the tomatoes occurs during the ripening process due to the relatively impermeable nature of the tomato skin. Ripening time will depend on the ripening temperature range however, ripening temperatures above 24°C will result in poor colour development with yellow or orange fruit rather than red. The heating and cooling capacity should be such that the tomatoes can be brought to the recommended ripening temperature within 24 hours.

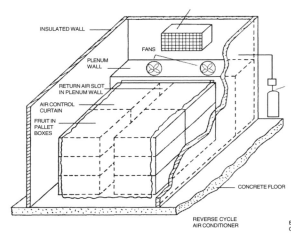

Figure 1: Tomato Ripening Room

General Arrangement

A typical arrangement for a tomato ripening room is shown in Figure 1 with the essential components of the system identified.

Room Size and Construction

For efficiency and convenience in operation, on-farm tomato ripening rooms are usually sized to accommodate the normal daily tomato pick during the peak harvest time. The room capacity is generally in the range of two to ten tonnes of tomatoes; however, larger rooms may sometimes be installed. Since the average ripening time is three or four days, the provision of multiple rooms on the one farm is generally desirable.

Air Circulation and Ventilation System

Fan-forced air circulation is required for adequate and uniform temperature control and ethylene gas distribution in the ripening room. An air circulation rate of two room air volumes per minute is recommended for good results. This is equivalent to around 480 cubic metres of air per hour per tonne of tomatoes. At the recommended heating or cooling capacity of 0.6 to 1.2kw per tonne of tomatoes, this gives an air temperature differential of 3.5 to 7°C across the heating or cooling system. These high air circulation rates are necessary to limit variations in temperature in different parts of the room to acceptable levels and to achieve an adequate rate of heating or cooling of the tomatoes.

The ventilation system circulates the room air continuously, introducing a small proportion of fresh air and exhausting a similar amount of air at the same time. This prevents a build up of ethylene gas in the room and also removes carbon dioxide produced by the fruit during respiration. If this carbon dioxide were allowed to build up to too high a level in the room atmosphere, it would interfere with the ripening process.

Temperature Control System

The temperature of tomatoes in the ripening room has a great influence on the ripening process. In fact, the product heat load usually represents around 80% of the total heat load. The remainder is due to heat transmission through the external walls of the room and the fresh air exchange rate. In some cases, both heating and cooling are required to maintain the room temperature within the required range. The time required for ripening can be reduced to some extent by increasing the temperature. Reverse cycle air-conditioners are successfully used for both heating and cooling in tomato-ripening rooms where humidity control does not appear to be of great importance.

Supply and Control Systems

With the trickled ethylene gas system, a low concentration of ethylene gas is maintained in the ripening room atmosphere by a continuous small, controlled flow of gas of about 10 parts per million (ppm). Ethylene gas is supplied as bottled gas under high pressure and it is released into the ripening room through a pressure regulator and metering system.

The outlet gas pressure is adjusted by means of the gas pressure regulator and the gas flow rate is then adjusted by the fine needle valve. A normally closed solenoid valve in the ethylene gas supply line ensures that gas is not discharged into the room unless the fans and ventilation system in the ripening room are operating. The solenoid valve is electrically interlocked with the operation of the ventilation system fans and is also controlled by an air flow switch. A gas control thermostat is used to measure when gas should be supplied to the room. The temperature-sensing element of this thermostat is pushed into a tomato so that it senses the pulp temperature of the tomatoes in different parts of the room.

Provided that the ethylene gas supply and control systems are correctly arranged, the ethylene gas concentration in the room will not exceed the low level which is sufficient for ripening but is far below the explosion hazard level. Under these conditions, tomato-ripening rooms installed on farms and used only for ripening fruit produced by the owner have been approved by certain Electricity Commissions as not constituting a hazardous location.

(Adapted from an article written by Brian Hesse for the 'Electrofarming Notebook' for The South East Queensland Electricity Board, October 1989.)

Questions 14 - 16

Complete the table in the box below.
*Use **NO MORE THAN THREE WORDS OR A NUMBER** for each answer. Write your answers in boxes 14 – 16 on your Answer Sheet.*

Requirements for successful use of the Ethylene Gas System for Tomato Ripening:

14 Tomatoes should be picked when they are ....

15 Room temperature must be .... °C.

16 Optimal ripening temperature for fruit must be achieved ....

Questions 17 - 20

Complete the flow chart below using information from the text.
*Use **NO MORE THAN THREE WORDS** for each answer. Write your answers in boxes 17 – 20 on your Answer Sheet.*

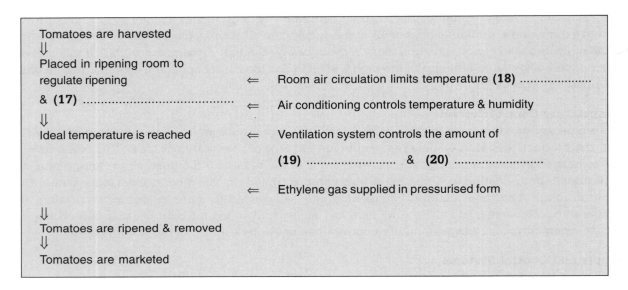

Tomatoes are harvested
⇓
Placed in ripening room to
regulate ripening   ⇐   Room air circulation limits temperature **(18)** ....
& **(17)** ....   ⇐   Air conditioning controls temperature & humidity
⇓
Ideal temperature is reached   ⇐   Ventilation system controls the amount of
                                          (19) .... & **(20)** ....

                                      ⇐   Ethylene gas supplied in pressurised form

⇓
Tomatoes are ripened & removed
⇓
Tomatoes are marketed

Questions 21 – 27

Below is a list of assumptions.
Using the information given in the passage, choose:

TRUE	*TRUE, if it is a reasonable assumption*
FALSE	*FALSE, if it is NOT a reasonable assumption*
NOT GIVEN	*if it is not possible to make the assumption from the information in the text.*

Write your answers in boxes 21 - 27 on your Answer Sheet.

		Answer
Example:	Ethylene gas systems improve the grower's chance of selling the tomatoes.	TRUE

21   Carbon dioxide is not beneficial to the ripening process.   ....

22   The outside air temperature determines the amount of extra heating needed
     in the ripening room.   ....

23   Increased temperature can speed up the maturing process.   ....

24   For successful tomato ripening, humidity levels need to be
      carefully monitored.   ....

25   The solenoid valve has to be checked at regular intervals.   ....

26   A build up of ethylene gas may result in an explosion.   ....

27   Setting up ethylene gas ripening rooms is not always safe.   ....

READING PASSAGE 3

Questions 28 - 40 are based on Reading Passage 3.

 ECO-TOURISM

If you still believe the once-commonly held misconception that tourism is only an indulgence for the wealthy, you are out of step with the times! The tourism market is accessible to, and indeed marketed toward, many different sections of the community. Adventurers, fitness freaks, nature-lovers and business people all contribute to a rapidly expanding sector of the global economy.

Section A
This billion-dollar industry, whilst affected slightly by the unforeseen events of 11 September 2001, has experienced significant growth since the late 1980s. The subsequent economic benefits for governments are well-documented as tourism boosts foreign investment and foreign exchange. Large-scale resorts and civil infrastructure were often the only response to successful marketing and increased tourist demand. It is not surprising then that the direct impact on the environment and regional or indigenous populations became a contentious issue. Governments and big business became the target of environmentalists and activists who argued that mass tourism was not (and is not) sustainable. As hordes of tourists descended on often overcrowded beaches and overused parklands, this became apparent. Eco-tourism was born.

Section B
The broad concept of eco-tourism as a nature-based, culturally sensitive form of tourism was taken up enthusiastically because there appeared to be few losers. Governments were given a convenient escape route as eco-tourism appeased the environmentalists and local communities, but still provided income. Environmentalists saw eco-tourism as an alternative to mass tourism and its resource-exploiting ways. Local communities envisaged receiving at least a percentage of the tourist dollars, creating job opportunities and giving them control over the impact on their own communities. It seemed that the benefits of mass tourism were going to be expanded in the new world of eco-tourism to include cultural, social and environmental elements.

Section C
As evidence of the benefits of eco-tourism unfolded, the practice has spread. So much so that the United Nations nominated 2002 as the International Year of Eco-tourism. Perhaps inevitably, the meaning of eco-tourism became less clear as it enveloped the globe. It could be argued that the form of eco-tourism adopted in some cases was found wanting in certain aspects and the need for agreement on a tighter definition resulted.

The eco-tourist is one who does not wish to contribute to the negative impact of large-scale tourism. He / she generally travels in small groups to low-key developments and attempts to "tread lightly" on the earth. These smaller-scale developments are environmentally responsible with a view to sustainability in all of the resources used. Their landscaping often relies on the use of native flora and they incorporate recycling methods and energy-efficient practices.

Within the eco-tourist's holiday experience will be an element of education about the local environment. The emphasis is on conservation and the part that humans play in keeping ecosystems functioning. If the area is of cultural or social importance, this too is highlighted.

The eco-tourist doesn't condone the exploitation of the indigenous or local community. Far from it, they insist that the host culture is acknowledged and respected. The repatriation of funds to external sources is frowned upon. Wherever possible, the benefits of an eco-tourist's holiday should be shared with the regional community — the hosts.

Section D

All of these elements promote minimal impact on human resources as well as on physical, cultural and environmental ones. They support conservation through education and experience. Despite the best of intentions, as popularity of eco-tourism spreads there is concern that the eco-tourist will have a more adverse effect on the environment.

Critics argue that unethical tour operators wanting to take advantage of the trendy eco-tourism market print brochures that espouse the ethics of eco-tourism and show familiar emblems of green frogs and crocodiles to promote themselves but do little else. If such operators are not held accountable, the industry will not survive. Open and honest eco-tourism marketing as well as world-recognised accreditation must be endorsed and implemented.

The sheer volume of tourists wanting to visit unique, unspoiled environments is also a cause for concern. Evidence of the need to restrict the number of visitors to sensitive areas exists in many eco-tourist attractions already. Hikers and bush walkers in Mount Kenya National Park have caused damage by straying from set trails and leaving food scraps behind. The number of Orca whales visiting Canada has declined in recent migratory seasons, as the restrictions placed on whale-watching boats and organisers are thought to be inadequate.

Section E

Eco-tourism does not guarantee sustainable tourism and it should not be viewed as a complete cure for the problems that have beset tourism. Until all stakeholders agree to a definition of eco-tourism, insist that eco-tourism operators abide by a strict code of ethics and carefully monitor the impact of eco-tourism (and all tourism), fragile ecosystems will continue to be besieged by tourists. There must be an educational program to promote ecologically-sustainable tourism across the board, so that the underlying principle in ALL forms of tourism is the management of resources.

Eco-tourism can bring wealth to areas where there is nothing else but natural attractions. The reasons for visiting The Galapagos Islands in Ecuador can only be explained by an interest in nature itself. The subsequent tourist dollars, if re-injected into the community, can mean the survival of such habitats. Licenses and entry fees to some sites have, in many cases, replaced government funding as their source of income.

Countries as diverse as Australia, New Zealand, Costa Rica and Kenya are developing strategies to identify and cope with the constraints that inevitably come with a long-term vision of sustainable tourism. Eco-tourism has played an important role in developing an awareness for sustainable tourism practices but governments, tourist agencies and operators must be willing to join forces with eco-tourists to ensure that natural attractions are protected from their own popularity.

Questions 28 – 31

Look at the list of headings (I – VI) below. Choose the most suitable headings for Sections B to E. Write your answers in boxes 28 - 31 on your Answer Sheet.

LIST OF HEADINGS
I   Eco-tourism Explained
II   The Appeal of Eco-tourism
III   Tourism Gives Birth to Eco-tourism
IV   The Future of Eco-tourism
V   Questioning Sustainability
VI   The Eco-tourist's Itinerary

Answer

Example:	Section A	...III....
28	Section B	....
29	Section C	....
30	Section D	....
31	Section E	....

Questions 32 – 36

Complete the sentences below with words taken from Reading Passage 3.
Use **NO MORE THAN THREE WORDS** for each answer. Write the answers in boxes 32 – 36 on your Answer Sheet.

32   Polluted, high density tourist destinations are proof that .... cannot be allowed to continue.

33   Eco-tourism spread because .... were obvious to environmental and government representatives as well as cultural and social groups.

34   Eco-tourists choose to stay in .... that do relatively less harm to the environment.

35   .... can damage the eco-tourism industry and governments need to supervise them carefully.

36   The success of the Galapagos Islands shows that .... can be a magnet for tourists.

Questions 37 – 40

Choose the correct letter from **A - D** and write it in boxes 37 – 40 on your Answer Sheet.

37   The main aim of the writer is to

   A   point out the economic benefits of tourism.
   B   outline the impact of tourism on the environment.
   C   introduce the concept of eco-tourism.
   D   explain the origins of eco-tourism.

38   The tourism industry cannot survive unless it

   A   promotes ecologically-sustainable activities.
   B   ensures that eco-tourism operators are genuine.
   C   considers the long-term effects of tourism on physical resources.
   D   All of the above.

39   The eco-tourist

   A   is often a victim of false advertising by unethical tour operators.
   B   accepts the restrictions that are placed on natural habitats.
   C   can unintentionally contribute to the negative effects of tourism.
   D   never goes to larger-scale tourist resorts.

40   The eco-tourism market

   A   is more likely to impact on natural habitats.
   B   is likely to restrict marketing of unethical tour operators.
   C   is more likely to repatriate profits from local communities.
   D   is likely to be more sustainable than mass tourism.

PRACTICE TEST 1 - WRITING

WRITING TASK 1

You should spend about 20 minutes on this task.

> *Tourism in the United Kingdom contributes billions of pounds sterling to the UK economy. The table below identifies the twelve most visited paid-admission attractions in the UK in 1999 and 2000.*
>
> *Write a report describing the information shown in the table.*

You should write at least 150 words.

The Top Most Visited Paid-Admission Attractions in the UK 1999 & 2000

Attraction	Location	Country	Visits 2000	Visits 1999	% Change
Millennium Dome	London	England	6,516,874E	Not opened yet	N/A
British Airways London Eye	London	England	3,300,000E	Not opened yet	N/A
Alton Towers	Alton	England	2,450,000	2,650,000	-7.5
Madame Tussaud's	London	England	2,388,000	2,640,000	-9.5
Tower of London	London	England	2,303,167	2,428,603	-5.2
Natural History Museum	London	England	1,577,044	1,696,725	-7.1
Chessington World of Adventures	Chessington	England	1,500,000E	1,550,000E	-3.2
Legoland Windsor	Windsor	England	1,490,000	1,620,000	-8.0
Victoria & Albert Museum	London	England	1,344,113	1,251,396	7.4
Science Museum	London	England	1,337,432	1,483,234	-9.8
Flamingo Land Theme Park & Zoo	Kirby Misperton	England	1,301,000E	1,197,000E	8.7
Canterbury Cathedral	Canterbury	England	1,263,140E	1,318,065E	-4.2

E = Estimated   N/A = Not Applicable

(Source: Sightseeing in UK, published by the National Tourism Boards. Permission granted for reproduction by English Tourism Council.)

WRITING TASK 2

You should spend about 40 minutes on this task.

Present a written argument to an educated reader with no specialist knowledge of the following topic:

> *Discuss when, if ever, capital punishment can be viewed as a valid punishment for crime.*

You should use your own ideas, knowledge and experience and support your arguments with examples and relevant evidence.

You should write at least 250 words.

PRACTICE TEST 1 - SPEAKING

▶ **PART 1:** (4 – 5 minutes) Introduction and (getting to know you) interview

Examiner: *Good morning. My name's ....*
And your name is...? And you're from... ?
Can I see your passport please? Thank you.

- *Which part of ..... are you from?*
- *Can you describe your hometown for me?*
- *Who do you live with?*
- *Do you spend much time with your family?*
- *What do you like to do on the weekend?*
- *Why are you studying English?*
- *How long have you been studying English?*

Thank you.

▶ **PART 2:** (3 – 4 minutes) Individual long turn (monologue)

Examiner: *Now I'm going to give you a card with some information about **FAMOUS PEOPLE**.*
*You will have one minute to read the card and then I'd like you to talk about **FAMOUS***
***PEOPLE** for one or two minutes. You can make some notes to help you if you wish. All right?*

Describe a famous person that has / had great influence on the people of your country.

    You should say:

    who that person was

    what that person did

    how you feel about that person

...and consider whether or not that person will continue to be an influence in the future.

Examiner: *Would you like to start now?*

You give your talk and after 1 or 2 minutes the examiner will ask you a question or two.

- *What would you do if you met that famous person?*
- *Do you think you'll ever be famous?*

Thank you.

▶ **PART 3:** (4 – 5 minutes) Two way discussion (more abstract conversation)

Examiner: *Now I'd like to ask you a few more questions.*

- *Famous people often become role models for teenagers. How significant is this?*
- *Do actors and models get too much attention in the media?*
- *Should people lose the right to privacy just because they are famous?*
- *If you could meet anyone famous (dead or alive) who would it be and why?*
- *In your opinion, do certain personality types handle fame or attention better than others?*
- *Do you feel that there should be restrictions placed on actors according to their age or sex?*

Thank you very much.
That's the end of the speaking test. Goodbye.

PRACTICE TEST 2 - LISTENING

SECTION 1: QUESTIONS 1 – 10

Listen to the conversation between an external student and a Receptionist at Grisham College Counselling Office.

Questions 1 – 3

Complete the Student Profile below.
*Use **NO MORE THAN THREE WORDS OR A NUMBER** for each answer.*

STUDENT PROFILE - GRISHAM COLLEGE

Example:

    A New student
    B Current student
    C Past student - graduate

    ANSWER: **B**

Student Number: **(1)** .... - EXT

Name: Jack LARASSY   **Course**: Master of Linguistics
                                        School of Languages & Literacy

Date of Birth: **(2)** .... / .... / 1979

Address: **(3)** .... Avenue
            CHELMSFORD, CM3 94Y

Questions 4 - 5

Complete the sign on the door of Grisham College Counselling Office below.
*Use **NO MORE THAN TWO WORDS OR A NUMBER** for each answer.*

Welcome to Student Services – Counselling Office

Office Hours: 8 a.m. to **(4)** ....

After Hours Entry: Use the **(5)** ....

                     and a Counsellor will let you in.

Telephone – 7893 4611

Listen to the conversation between the same student and the Student Counsellor.

Questions 6 – 10

Complete the Counsellor's notes.

Student Name:	**Jack LARASSY**
Current Job	**Possible Future Job**
- working as a **(6)** .... - studying part-time	- research at university
Likes - the satisfaction - the six week summer holiday	**Advantages** - **(8)** .... teaching - increase in pay - would still have **(9)** .... - professionally beneficial
Dislikes - badly behaved students - lazy students - insufficient **(7)**	**Disadvantages** - **(10)** working .... - extra travel time

SECTION 2:   QUESTIONS 11 – 20

Questions 11 – 13

Choose the correct letter from **A - C** *for each answer.*

11   The problem that Constable Gray describes is

    A   women being robbed.
    B   thieves stealing bags from international tourists.
    C   Darlinghurst residents being robbed.

12   It is difficult to chase the thieves because

    A   they catch their victims by surprise.
    B   they choose older victims.
    C   the victims find it difficult to run as fast as the thieves.

13   The police have caught

    A   only two of the thieves.
    B   none of the thieves yet.
    C   almost all of the thieves.

Questions 14 - 15

Choose **TWO** *letters from* **A - E** *for each answer.*

14 & 15   Police advise the group of students to

    A   chase the thieves if it is safe.
    B   be more careful of where they place their bags.
    C   avoid being alone in the area.
    D   avoid carrying too much money with them.
    E   use credit cards as much as possible.

Questions 16 – 20.

Complete the following notes using **NO MORE THAN THREE WORDS** for each answer.

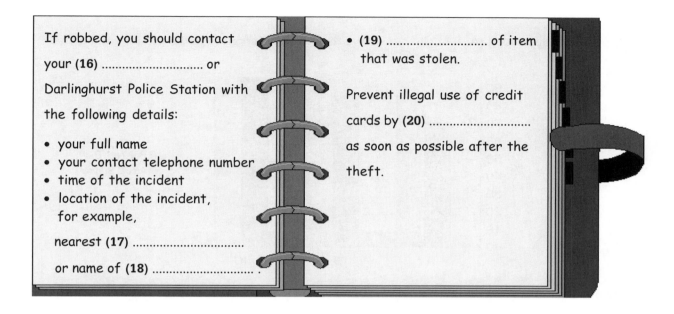

If robbed, you should contact your (16) .... or Darlinghurst Police Station with the following details:

- your full name
- your contact telephone number
- time of the incident
- location of the incident, for example,

  nearest (17) ....

  or name of (18) ....

- (19) .... of item that was stolen.

Prevent illegal use of credit cards by (20) .... as soon as possible after the theft.

SECTION 3: QUESTIONS 21 – 30

Questions 21 - 25

Choose the correct letter from **A - C** for each answer.

21 What is the purpose of Jane and Rick's meeting with the tutor?

    A To collate information from their assignments
    B To follow the correct procedure for the report
    C To check on details of the report

22 What work still needs to be completed before doing the presentation?

    A Conducting the actual questionnaire survey
    B Collating data from the questionnaire and writing the report itself
    C Analyzing the information gathered in the questionnaire

23 Which chart **A**, **B** or **C** shows the correct distribution of the 400 surveys Jane and Rick handed out?

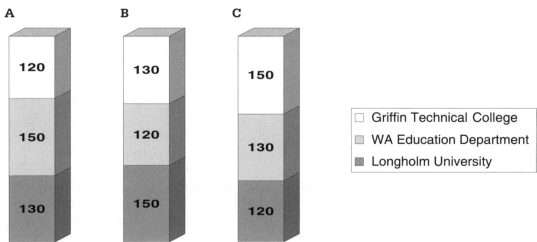

24 Why did Jane and Rick survey international students from three different institutions?

    A They didn't want to limit their responses to Longholm.
    B There weren't enough international students at Longholm.
    C They could access students of different ages at other institutions.

25 Which illustration (**A, B** or **C**) best shows the rates of responses in the pre-test and actual survey?

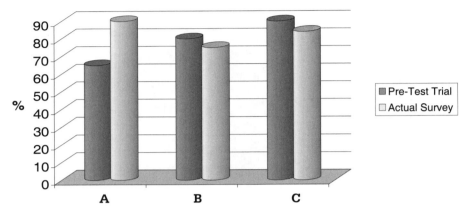

Questions 26 - 30

*Complete the following flow chart. Insert the steps **A – F** given in the box below.*

NOTE: *there are more steps than you will need.*

STEPS:

    A Distribute transmittal letter   **E** Present pre-test trial results
    B Rewrite unclear items   **F** Draw conclusions
    C Compile trial survey report   **G** Set objectives
    D Send reminders for overdue surveys

Steps for Survey and Presentation:

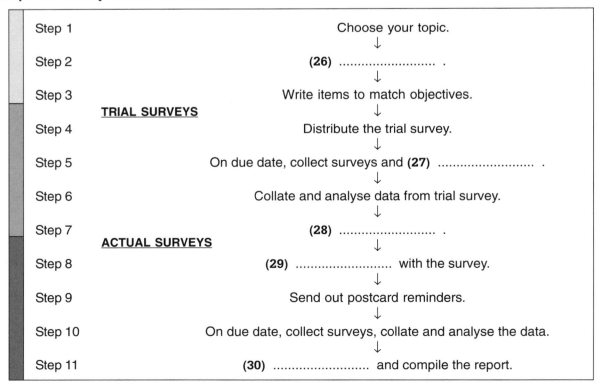

Step 1	Choose your topic.
Step 2	**(26)** ....
Step 3	Write items to match objectives.
TRIAL SURVEYS	
Step 4	Distribute the trial survey.
Step 5	On due date, collect surveys and **(27)** ....
Step 6	Collate and analyse data from trial survey.
Step 7	**(28)** ....
ACTUAL SURVEYS	
Step 8	**(29)** .... with the survey.
Step 9	Send out postcard reminders.
Step 10	On due date, collect surveys, collate and analyse the data.
Step 11	**(30)** .... and compile the report.

SECTION 4:   QUESTIONS 31 – 40

Questions 31 - 34

Complete the summary below.
*Use **NO MORE THAN THREE WORDS** for each answer.*

> **PROJECT MANAGEMENT**
>
> Last week's definition of project management:
>
> Project Management has
>
> - a clear **(31)** ....
>
> - goals, budget and **(32)** ....
>
> A project can be divided into **(33)** ....
>
> The subject of today's lecture is **(34)** ....

Questions 35 - 39

Complete the table below.
*Use **NO MORE THAN THREE WORDS** for each answer.*

Elements of Stage 2	Considerations
Budget Planning	- most challenging element - try to plan **(35)** ....
Allocation of Time	- dependent on **(36)** .... - **(37)** .... used to identify tasks and schedules in units of work
(38)	- outlined in tender documents - help for this element can be obtained from **(38)** .... Manager

Question 40

Complete the sentence below.
*Use **NO MORE THAN THREE WORDS** for the answer.*

40 The three elements of Stage 2 will be examined in more depth in ....

PRACTICE TEST 2 - READING

READING PASSAGE 1

Questions 1 - 13 are based on Reading Passage 1.

Poverty and Health

The link between health and economic outcomes has always been a central issue for both economists and sociologists. Most experts believe that there is a strong causal link between health and economic prosperity. For example, those earning higher incomes have more money to invest in human capital such as improving and maintaining health. This means that their standard of living improves as their earning power increases and they are able to invest in better diets, improved sanitation and better health care. A healthy worker is less likely to contract disease, and this means productivity at work improves with the resultant opportunity to command higher earnings.

A clear example of the link between economic productivity and poor health is Uganda, which is situated in the east of central Africa. Recent surveys have indicated that 46% of the population is forced to live on less than $1.00 per day. Only 49% of households in Uganda have access to health care facilities. The current average life expectancy is 48 years from birth, which is estimated to be about 45 for males and 50.5 years for females. An assessment of the burden of disease in Uganda in 1995 demonstrated that 75% of life years lost as a result of premature death were due to entirely preventable diseases: perinatal and maternal conditions accounted for 20%; malaria for 15.4%; acute lower respiratory tract infections 10.5%; AIDS 9.1%; diarrhoea 8.4%. In addition, 38% of under five year olds are stunted, 25% are underweight and 5% wasted. These factors accounted for the extremely high mortality rate experienced in this age-group.

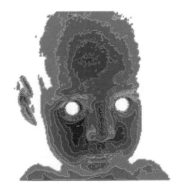

A recent report from Healthcare Worldwide makes the clearest and strongest case yet that disease has a fundamental and disastrous effect on the economies of countries and, in the long run, at the global level. The report concludes that funding increases for health from affluent and poorer countries alike are vital. Although the extra expenditure from poorer countries would be difficult to find, the report concluded that the benefits received would be worth it. It is estimated that this injection of funds into the healthcare systems of the poorer countries would result in a significant increase in productivity because people would be healthier and more able to work. The report also urges a focus on the biggest killers, from childbirth and AIDS, and on medical care at a local clinic level rather than in prestigious hospitals.

To this end, the Ugandan government has pursued a comprehensive poverty reduction strategy which has addressed the issues of access to appropriate and adequate health care by utilising the existing political structure of the country. This strategy has resulted in the incidence of poverty in Uganda falling from 56% in 1992 to 35% in 2000. The Multinational Finance Corporation (MFC) has praised the East African country for the progress it has made towards reducing poverty and has just announced its approval of a staggered $21 million loan which will be made available in three equal parts over three years beginning in 2002.

This incentive means that Uganda has become the first country this year to benefit from a Poverty Reduction Support Credit (PRSC). This is a new approach to World Bank lending, available exclusively to low-income countries with strong policy and institutional reform programs, which allows poverty reduction strategies to be carried out.

However, the MFC notes that although the Ugandan economy has performed relatively well during 2001-2002 in achieving a 5.5% growth, Uganda would still continue to rely heavily on donor assistance. The United Nations Human Development Report for 2002 ranks Uganda as 150th out of 173 countries, and reports it is "far behind" in its attempts to gain the anticipated 10% increase. It may also be unable to reach the hoped for Millennium Development goal of halving the proportion of people suffering from hunger by 2015.

The Ugandan government is also dedicated to the control of AIDS through the Uganda AIDS Commission. In 1993, Uganda reported the highest rate of AIDS cases per population in Africa and, therefore, the world. HIV, the name given to the preliminary stages of AIDS, and AIDS, the fully developed form of the disease, are still one of the leading causes of death in Uganda. Currently, about 2.4 million people in the country are HIV positive while another 0.9 million have the fully developed form. To make matters worse, the majority of those affected with the disease are within the 15 and 40 year age group, which is where the majority of the labour force comes from. Therefore the economy suffers. However, since the introduction of the Uganda AIDS Commission, there has been a major decrease in the incidence of the disease.

The struggle to maintain adequate and appropriate levels of health care in underdeveloped countries will continue to represent a major challenge to organizations such as Healthcare Worldwide and UNICEF. However, through the involvement of the more affluent countries and the development of a global fund set up by the United Nations, hope is present and there is an air of optimism about the future.

Questions 1 - 3

Using information from Reading Passage 1, complete the diagram below.
*Use **NO MORE THAN THREE WORDS** for each answer. Write your answers in boxes 1 - 6 on your Answer Sheet.*

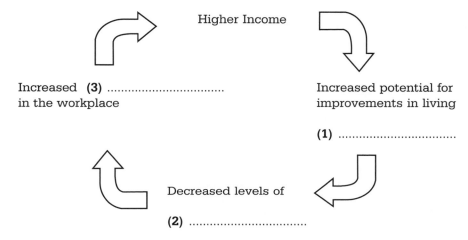

Higher Income

Increased **(3)** .... in the workplace

Increased potential for improvements in living

(1) ....

Decreased levels of

(2) ....

Questions 4 – 8

Complete the following table using information taken from Reading Passage 1.
*Use **NO MORE THAN THREE WORDS OR A NUMBER** for each answer. Write your answers in boxes 4 – 8 on your Answer Sheet.*

Households with no access to medical facilities	**(4)** ....
Deaths which were not preventable	**(5)** ....
Children who **(6)** .... less than they should	25%
MFC loan for use in 2002	**(7)** ....
The difference between the actual and **(8)** .... growth rate	4.5%

Figure 1. Facts on Uganda

Questions 9 – 13

Choose the correct letter from **A** *-* **D** *and write it in boxes 9 - 13 on your Answer Sheet.*

9   Poor health amongst Ugandans

   A results from insufficient acess to healthcare facilities.
   B can be attributed to poor economic conditions.
   C has resulted in increased mortality rates.
   D All of the above.

10   Healthcare Worldwide recommends

   A spending more money on health worldwide.
   B investigating the incidence of death due to childbirth and AIDS.
   C making health care facilities accessible at a local level.
   D All of the above.

11   The Poverty Reduction Support Credit

   A was first offered to Uganda.
   B is a department of the World Bank.
   C only helps certain low-income countries.
   D None of the above.

12   HIV/AIDS in Uganda

   A is not as prevalent as it used to be.
   B causes the highest rate of death in the world.
   C targets those who no longer work.
   D occurs in 2.4 million of the population.

13   The writer of this article

   A believes Uganda's situation will ultimately improve.
   B thinks that developed countries do not help Uganda enough.
   C is optimistic about the future in general.
   D is sympathetic to poorer countries.

READING PASSAGE 2

Questions 14 - 27 are based on Reading Passage 2.

VALIUM

 In the 1960s, Valium was launched around the world as the new miracle pill. It was prescribed for dozens of ailments, including stress, panic attacks, back pain, insomnia and calming patients before and after surgery. Four decades later, many are questioning why the drug is still so popular, given that doctors and drug addiction workers believe Valium, and drugs like it, create more health problems than they solve.

Valium – a Latin word meaning "strong and well" – was developed in the early 1960s in the United States (US) by Dr Leo Sternbach, a Polish chemist working for pharmaceutical giant Hoffman-LaRoche. Approved for use in 1963, Valium quickly became a favourite among mental heath professionals and general practitioners. Valium was the most prescribed drug in the US between 1969 and 1982. At the peak of Valium use in the 1970s, Hoffman LaRoche's parent company, the Roche Group, was selling about two billion Valium pills a year, earning the company $US 600 million a year. Valium quickly became a household name, the drug of choice for millions of people, from the rich and famous to the stressed executive and the frustrated housewife.

These days Valium is still a popular choice. From 2002-2003, 50% of prescriptions for diazepams (the generic name for Valium) in Australia were for Valium. Almost two million scripts were issued for diazepam in 2002, costing consumers and governments more than $13 million.

Diazepams belong to a class of drugs known as benzodiazepines, which include tranquillizers to ease anxiety and hypnotics to treat insomnia. Valium and other benzodiazepines were marketed as fast acting, non-addictive and as having no side effects. Initially benzodiazepines were considered to be quite safe, especially compared to other drugs on the market. For example, barbiturates were also very toxic and a small overdose would be fatal.

One of the great advantages of benzodiazepines over their predecessors was that even if the patient took many tablets, they would get very sick and go off to sleep, but they wouldn't die. It seemed too good to be true. And of course it was.

Some doctors began to observe alarming facts about benzodiazepines which weren't well known during the 1960s and the 1970s, and which are still true today. They were addictive, even in small doses; they could be safely prescribed for only a very short period; and the body adapted to the drug within a week, which usually led the user to take higher dosages or an increased number of tablets.

In addition to this, what wasn't well known until the early 1980s is that a much larger group of people had become dependent on these benzodiazepines, including Valium, by taking the normal dose. Although they were only taking 2 mg three times a day, doctors observed that within a week they were becoming dependent. Moreover, they were becoming very ill if that dose was reduced or withdrawn.

Because the withdrawal from benzodiazepines is brutal, doctors continue to prescribe the medication for fear of the patient's health during withdrawal. Doctors believe that there is no point in refusing to prescribe the drug until the patient is prepared to stop. Valium has a long half-life, which means that it takes 30-plus hours for the body to get rid of half of the daily dose. As a result, withdrawals from Valium are just as difficult as withdrawals from other drugs, including alcohol. Patients who are withdrawing can have fits for five or six days after they have stopped taking Valium, which is one of the big risks. It usually takes the body five to seven days to detoxify from alcohol and less than a month for heroin compared to withdrawal from Valium which can take up to six months.

Many doctors believe that Valium gives people false hope and argue that while many patients feel better when they initially begin taking the drug, the feelings are short-lived. In the case of benzodiazepines they should only be taken as part of an overall examination of the patient's lifestyle.

Guidelines have been developed to support the appropriate use by doctors and patients of Valium and other benzodiazepines. Doctors need to talk about what is causing the stress and suggest possible alternative treatment options. The flip side of the coin is that consumers need to take ownership of the medicines that they are taking. They should talk to their doctor about the impact the medication has on their health. This also helps doctors to help manage their patient's health. The emergence of concerns over the use of Valium, originally hailed as the wonder drug of its day, is a warning for us all to be cautious about the newer drugs. What it all boils down to is that doctors and patients need to monitor the use of all medicines – this includes prescription medicine as well as over-the-counter medications.

(Source: The Weekend Australian, Saturday 26 July 2003,"Anxious and Addicted" by Clare Pirani. Copyright: used with permission.)

Questions 14 – 18

Look at the following statements (Questions 14 - 18). Indicate:

YES	*if the statement agrees with information in the passage*
NO	*if the statement contradicts information in the passage*
NOT GIVEN	*if the information is not given in the passage*

Write your answers in boxes 14 - 18 on your Answer Sheet.

Answer

Example:	Valium was launched as a new miracle pill.	..**YES**..
14	Valium is of greater risk to users than their original illness.	....
15	Valium sales caused business in the Roche Group to peak in the 1970s.	....
16	Valium became popular because it seemed to suit a wide range of people.	....
17	Valium is part of the group of drugs called diazepams.	....
18	A Valium overdose is not fatal.	....

Questions 19 - 27

Complete the summary below by using words taken from Reading Passage 2.
*Use **NO MORE THAN THREE WORDS OR A NUMBER** for each answer. Write your answers in boxes 19 - 27 on your Answer Sheet.*

Initially, doctors believed that Valium was a comparatively **(19)** .... drug for a number of reasons: it worked quickly, patients could take it but give it up easily and it didn't create any unpleasant **(20)** ....

However, about thirty years ago some disturbing facts became apparent. Doctors found that Valium was **(21)** .... in the short term and users needed to **(22)** .... the dosage in order to get the same effect. They also found that even users who took a **(23)** .... dose became addicted very quickly. In addition to this, one of the most worrying concerns about Valium use was that it was extremely **(24)** .... for users to give up the drug because it had a long half-life. Doctors are now aware that patients who take Valium merely receive a short-lived feeling of **(25)** ....

Therefore, guidelines have been developed to make sure that it is used only when it is **(26)** .... More caution needs to be exercised. Doctors need to talk about patients' stress levels and advise them of **(27)** .... Finally, patients need to be more aware of the medications they take.

READING PASSAGE 3

Questions 28 - 40 are based on Reading Passage 3.

GLOBAL WARMING – THE BEGINNING OF THE END?

Increased social debate regarding complex issues such as The Greenhouse Effect and Global Warming has definitely increased our environmental awareness. However, such debates are often emotive rather than informative. One can be forgiven, for example, for believing that the Greenhouse Effect is something we should be trying to eradicate!

Short-wave radiation, in the form of visible ultra-violet (UV) light from the Sun, penetrates Earth's atmosphere to warm the surface of the planet. Because all matter is warmer than space, it radiates heat, and part of the sun's energy is re-radiated out by the Earth's surface. Greenhouse gases in the atmosphere trap some of this infrared radiation causing the Earth's surface and lower atmospheric layers to warm up to a higher temperature than would otherwise be the case. Without these greenhouse gases, Earth would be a frozen, hostile environment with an average global temperature of about $-15°$ C to $-19°$ C, where no life could be sustained. A thermal balance of energy exists where the Earth radiates about the same amount of energy into space as long-wave radiation that it absorbs from the sun. Our atmosphere allows the balance to be achieved because the trace gases trap and absorb heat.

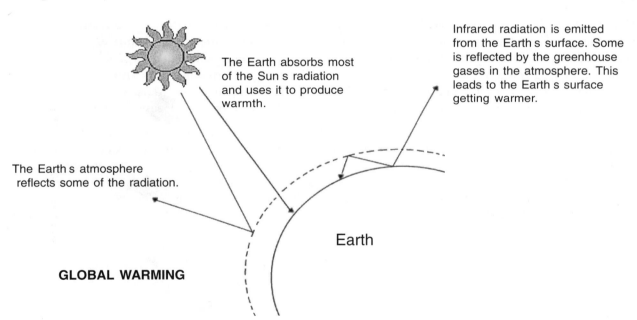

Other interactions are at play that may affect the Earth's albedo or balance of energy. The amount or type of cloud cover, for instance, can alter the amount of energy being exchanged. Cirrus clouds reflect more of the sun's radiation than absorb radiation from the earth. Cumulus clouds do the opposite where the proportion of energy retained is larger than that reflected.

The detected increase in carbon dioxide in our atmosphere since the Industrial Revolution will also affect the albedo. Not only has there been an increase in carbon dioxide identified. Other greenhouse base gases such as methane, nitrous oxide and chlorofluorocarbons have all increased. It is thought that the latter of these minor greenhouse gases may have a stronger impact on global warming than carbon dioxide levels.

The largest contributing factor to the increase of greenhouse gases has been the burning of fossil fuels. Carbon in the fuel we burn is oxidised and released into the atmosphere as carbon dioxide. Compounding the problem, deforestation that has taken place over the last 50 – 100 years reduces the number of trees that are necessary for absorbing carbon dioxide from the atmosphere. Short-term solutions for regional economic survival means the importance of rainforests in this gas exchange has been ignored. Even a layman can see how the Greenhouse Effect has earned its bad reputation. An out-of-control Greenhouse Effect is often quoted using the example of Venus, where heat is trapped by thick clouds and a dense carbon dioxide atmospheric element, making the surface temperature as high as 500° C.

Scientists don't always agree on their predictions. Whilst they agree that an increase in Greenhouse gases will cause the Earth's temperature to rise, they disagree on what may happen next. Some believe that the subsequent increase in water vapour may help to reduce the temperature. Others believe it will increase the temperature.The collection of meteorological data from observation satellites and a study of samples taken from glaciers and trees for example, support what many of planet Earth's inhabitants notice for themselves. The globe is warming up. It is generally agreed that by about 2030/2040, the average global temperature (presently +15° C) will have risen by anything up to 5° C causing polar ice-caps and mountain glaciers to melt and changes to ocean currents and circulation patterns causing coastal waters to rise. New weather patterns and extremes are anticipated.

Scientists do not know if the increase in average global temperature is just a cycle because of the absence of long-term meteorological data. Comparing climate epochs is complex because so many atmospheric and surface features of land and ocean are different. All of the elements that make up climate are continually changing and dynamically interacting. Knowing therefore, that the earth cooled during past ice ages and warmed during interglacial periods, has limited worth in predictions for our future. Moreover, records of past climatic epochs are not as reliable or detailed as those records developed in recent decades.

General Circulation Models (GCMs) are designed to describe basic behaviour patterns of the atmosphere. Used on super-computers, the system still cannot represent all countries and has to rely on spatial representation of the earth. This means that specific consequences of climate change – like predicting the daily weather for specific climatic regions – are more difficult to predict than the global reality of the Greenhouse Effect. The computers are much more accurate in showing these broader climatic conditions and predicting global effects than more localized phenomena.

Many experts conclude that failure to take action in order to limit the impact of human activity is taking a dangerous risk. Others argue that nature will save itself from our apparent inability or disinterest in protecting the planet and that adaptation will, once again, be the key to survival. As these debates continue and governments refuse to act, it is becoming more likely that we will be able to see for ourselves whether or not the dire predictions of global warming are overstated as early as the middle of this century.

―――――◆―――――

Questions 28 - 31

Complete the sentences below with words taken from the passage.
*Use **NO MORE THAN THREE WORDS OR A NUMBER** for each answer. Write your answers in boxes 28 - 31 on your Answer Sheet.*

28 The Earth's atmosphere would not be able to retain heat, were it not for ....

29 Clouds, as well as human activity, may contribute to an imbalance in the ....

30 A reduction in the amount of radiation going into space can be the result of .... clouds.

31 Carbon dioxide levels have increased due to the burning of fossil fuels and ....

Questions 32 - 35

Reading Passage 3 describes numerous cause and effect relationships.
Match each **EFFECT** with one of the **CAUSES** (*A – G*) below.

NOTE: there are more causes than you will need to use. You may use any cause more than once.

LIST OF CAUSES

A rise in water vapour
B rise in global temperature
C greenhouse gases
D thick cloud and carbon dioxide
E radiation
F reduction in number of trees
G holes in the ozone layer

CAUSE:

32 **EFFECT:** ineffective carbon dioxide exchange   ....

33 **EFFECT:** high increase in temperature of the land   ....

34 **EFFECT:** increase in water vapour   ....

35 **EFFECT:** possible increase or decrease in the temperature of the land   ....

Questions 36 – 40

Look at the following statements (Questions 36 - 40). Indicate:

TRUE   if the statement agrees with information in the passage
FALSE   if the statement contradicts information in the passage
NOT GIVEN   if the information is not given in the passage

Write your answers in boxes 36 - 40 on your Answer Sheet.

Answer

36   Over the next 30 years the average global temperature is expected
      to be at least 20°C.   ....

37   Long-term meteorological data confirms cyclical increases in average
      global temperatures.   ....

38   Historical climatic records are no longer used because of recent findings.   ....

39   GCMs are not reliable indicators of the specific consequences of
      climate change.   ....

40   If action is not taken now, governments will be forced to act by 2050.   ....

PRACTICE TEST 2 - WRITING

WRITING TASK 1

You should spend about 20 minutes on this task.

> *The bar chart below illustrates the use of tobacco products by secondary school students in the United States.*
>
> *Write a report describing the information shown.*

You should write at least 150 words.

Current Tobacco Use Among Middle and High School Students

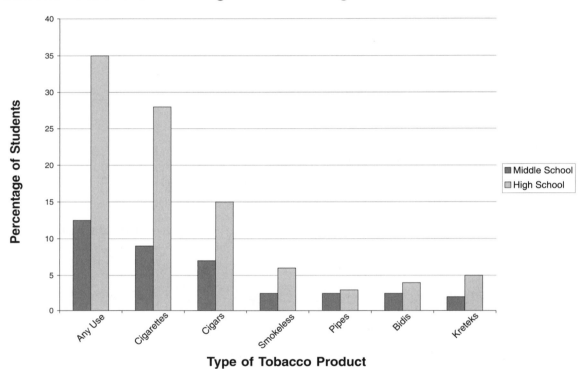

(Source: Centers for Disease Control & Prevention: National Center for Health Statistics: Health, US MMWR VOL48 #43. Permission granted by Office on Smoking and Health.)

WRITING TASK 2

You should spend about 40 minutes on this task.

Present a written argument to an educated reader with no specialist knowledge on the following topic:

> *The percentage of overweight children in western society has increased by almost 20% in the last ten years. Discuss the possible causes and effects of this disturbing trend and offer a solution.*

You should use your own ideas, knowledge and experience and support your arguments with examples and relevant evidence.

You should write at least 250 words.

PRACTICE TEST 2 - SPEAKING

▶ **PART 1:** (4 – 5 minutes) Introduction and (getting to know you) interview

Examiner: *Good morning. My name's ……….*
And your name is…? And you're from… ?
Can I see your passport please? Thank you.

- *Which part of…(your country)…are you from?*
- *Can you describe your hometown for me?*
- *What do you like about living in…(your country)?*
- *Do you work or are you a student?*
- *What do you like to do in your spare time?*
- *Why are you studying English?*
- *How long have you been studying English?*

Thank you.

▶ **PART 2:** (3 – 4 minutes) Individual long turn (monologue)

Examiner: *Thanks. Now I'm going to give you a card with some information about* **TRANSPORT***.*
You will have one minute to read the card and then I'd like you to talk about **TRANSPORT**
for one or two minutes. You can make some notes to help you if you wish. All right?

Describe the main forms of transport in your hometown.

You should say:

what the different forms of transport are

how often you use them

which types of transport are most popular

…and consider whether or not the transportation systems are satisfactory.

Examiner: *Would you like to start now?*

You give your talk and after 1 or 2 minutes the examiner will ask you a question or two.

- *Do you prefer travelling by public transport or by car?*
- *What's the longest journey you have ever been on?*

Thank you.

▶ **PART 3:** (4 – 5 minutes) Two way discussion (more abstract conversation)

Examiner: *Now I'd like to ask you a few more questions.*

- *What is the traffic like in your hometown?*
- *What are the benefits of travelling by public transport?*
- *In your opinion, in what ways can governments encourage people to use public transport?*
- *Having too many cars on our roads causes air pollution. What are some of the other causes of pollution?*
- *How are environmentally-friendly practices encouraged in (your country)?*
- *Science can be used to develop environmentally-friendly alternatives. In what ways can this be done?*

Thank you very much.
That's the end of the speaking test. Goodbye.

PRACTICE TEST 3 - LISTENING

SECTION 1:   QUESTIONS 1 – 10

Listen to the conversation between two friends who are talking outside an examination room.

Questions 1 – 2

*Choose the correct letter from **A - C** for each answer.*

> *Example:* Why is Peter tired?
>
> **A**   The exam was long.
> **B**   He got up early this morning.
> **C**   He studied until late the previous night.
>
> ANSWER: **C**

1   Why can't Peter relax over the three-week vacation?

   A   He needs to earn some money.
   B   He's worried about next semester.
   C   He can't afford to go away.

2   What does Crystal plan to do on the holidays?

   A   She's going to visit her family.
   B   She's going to get a job.
   C   She hasn't got any idea.

Questions 3 – 5

Listen to the directions and identify the place names of Questions 3 – 5 on the campus map below. Choose your answers from the list of place name in the boxes.
NOTE: *there are more place names listed than you will need.*

List of Place Names:	I Block
	C Block
	Student Employment Office
	Student Canteen
	Bookshop

3   ....

4   ....

5   ....

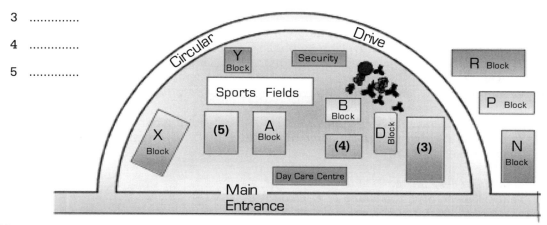

Questions 6 – 7

Complete the sentences below.
Use **NO MORE THAN THREE WORDS OR A NUMBER** *for each answer.*

6   First, Peter and Crystal must have a/an ....

7   Peter and Crystal arrange to meet at .... on Friday.

Questions 8 - 10

Complete the table below.
Use **NO MORE THAN ONE WORD OR A NUMBER** *for each answer.*

	Surname	Contact Phone Number	Student Number
Peter	(8)	(9)	B 723466
Crystal	LU	~	(10) ....

SECTION 2:   QUESTIONS 11 – 20

Questions 11 – 13

*Choose the correct letter from **A - C** for each answer.*

11   The main aim of the festival spokesperson at the gathering is to
    A   welcome visitors to Brisbane.
    B   give away some tickets to the Brisbane Festival.
    C   provide information regarding the Festival.

12   The program for the Brisbane Festival includes performers from
    A   local and international destinations.
    B   Australian, Asian and European destinations.
    C   Australian and international destinations.

13   The Brisbane Festival will schedule activities and performances
    A   at indoor and outdoor venues.
    B   over 290 days.
    C   in traditional performance centres around the city.

Questions 14 – 20

Complete the table below.
Use **NO MORE THAN THREE WORDS OR A NUMBER** *for each answer.*

Type of Activity	Date	Time	Name of Event	Venue
Music	8 Sept	8 p.m.	Israel Philharmonic Orchestra	Performing Arts Centre
Drama	(14)	6:30 p.m.	Monkey	Power House
(15)	11 Sept	8 p.m.	Sumi Jo with Queensland Orchestra	Performing Arts Centre
Music	Wed - Sat	~	(16)	City Gardens
Visual Arts	From (17)	~	Asia-Pacific Triennial	Art Gallery
Drama	15 Sept	6 p.m.	Slava's Snowshow	(18) ....
Music	20 Sept	8 p.m.	Barbara Fordham in concert	(19) ....
Poetry	From 22 Sept	~	Poetry Festival	~
Writing	4 Oct - 6 Oct	~	Writers' Festival	~
Music	6 Oct	6 p.m.	(20) Opera	City Gardens

SECTION 3:   QUESTIONS 21 – 30

Question 21

Choose the correct letter from **A - C** *for each answer.*

21   Who are Nancy and Jenny?
   A   Students from Singapore and Malaysia
   B   Students who have travelled to Singapore and Malaysia
   C   Students who have researched Singapore and Malaysia

Questions 22 – 24

Complete the table below.
*Use **NO MORE THAN THREE WORDS OR A NUMBER** for each answer.*

COUNTRY PROFILES		
	Singapore	**Malaysia**
Area of land:	630 square kilometres	**(22)** .... square kilometres
Population:	**(23)**	Under 24 million
Approximate ethnic mix:	**(24)** .... Chinese 14% Malay 9% Indian	65% Malay (Bumiputera) 26% Chinese 8% Indian

Questions 25 – 30

Complete the sentences below.
*Use **NO MORE THAN THREE WORDS** for each answer.*

25   Australia's relationship with Singapore has been ....

26   Trade between Singapore and Australia is ....

27   Singapore and Malaysia share .... and .... as their top trading partners.

28   There has been an increase in .... between Australia and Malaysia.

29   Nancy found that the government in Singapore invested a lot in ....

30   Nancy and Jenny thought that Malaysia has a good balance of .... customs.

SECTION 4:   QUESTIONS 31 – 40

Questions 31 - 32

Complete the notes below.
*Use **NO MORE THAN THREE WORDS** for each answer.*

31   For .... there have been vegetarians.

32   True vegans will only eat food which ....

Questions 33 - 34

*Choose **TWO** letters from **A - E** for each answer.*

33 & 34   Which two reasons are NOT given in the lecture for adopting vegetarianism?

    A   religious beliefs
    B   environmental reasons
    C   peer pressure
    D   cost
    E   social acceptance

Questions 35 - 36

Choose **TWO** letters from **A - E** for each answer.

35 & 36 Which two health issues are NOT used in the lecture to promote vegetarianism as healthy?

      A   reduced heart disease
      B   lower risk of contracting cancer
      C   reduced blood sugar levels
      D   fewer weight-related problems
      E   lower risk of stomach ulcers

Questions 37 – 39

Complete the following table.
Use **NO MORE THAN THREE WORDS** *for each answer.*

VITAMIN AND MINERAL INTAKE

	Available to non-vegetarians in...	Available to most vegetarians in...	Available to lacto-vegetarians and vegans in...
Iron	meat	spinach, prune juice or (37)	~
B12	meat, fish and dairy products	dairy or soy products and (38)	vegetable margarines, soy products and some (39) ....

Question 40

Complete the sentence below.
Write **NO MORE THAN THREE WORDS** *for your answer.*

40 The website address given for the UK Vegetarian Society is ....

PRACTICE TEST 3 - READING

READING PASSAGE 1

Questions 1 - 13 are based on Reading Passage 1.

COMPUTER SECURITY

It is believed that the problem of computer security has changed over a period of time as businesses, through an increased use of information technology (IT), have become more and more dependent on information and the associated information systems (IS). However, at the same time, there has been limited change in the implemented security or safeguards to these information systems. In fact many executives or managers fail to even identify the relevant requirement for security or policies.

A. The Internet has been roughly doubling in size every year, and the associated security incidents have been running in parity. Even if the percentage of malicious users is small, the increase in size of the Internet and in the number of incidents of failed security is significant. The importance of the growth in the Internet can be highlighted by the fact that in July 1991, 33% of Internet users were from the commercial sector, whereas in July 1996, this figure had risen to 50%.

B. In 1988, the Morris 'worm' was introduced on the Internet to invade, attack and replicate itself on the network. The response was to shut down E-mail and connectivity. However, the 'fixes' were to be distributed via E-mail and so the solution was self-defeating. As a result of this worm virus, CERT (Computer Emergency Response Team) was formed, with the Australian version (AUSCERT) starting in 1992.

C. One of the problems with Internet security is the fact that the incidents are increasing in sophistication. One of the reasons for this has been the increasing availability of toolkits. Although these toolkits are designed to assist computer systems designers to protect and develop their sites, they also allow relatively ignorant intruders to carry out increasingly complex incidents with the utilisation of many routers and disguises to reach their 'target'. According to a US Department of Defence report, less than 1% of incidents are identified but 65% of these are successful. Another thing to bear in mind with intruders and hackers is that they do not respect geographical or administrative boundaries, or time zones. They may be geographically dislocated from the point of attack and therefore operating in 'off-duty' hours.

D. The thing to remember with security is that the system administrators must get it right all the time; the intruder must get it right just once. Evidence of this is easy to find. In 1997, a teenager hacked into a Bell Atlantic network. His hacking crashed the computer and resulted in 600 homes, a regional airport and emergency services being without telephone communications for six hours. And what was the punishment for this offence? Two years probation, community service and a fine of US$5,000.

E. Governments are getting tough on cyber crimes, especially in the wake of September 11th. These crimes are being linked to national security, which in the US is now of major concern to government officials and the general public alike. And the government has been swift to act. In late 2001, the US Patriot Act was introduced. This Act increased the maximum sentence for breaking into a computer from five to ten years. Then in July 2002, the House of Representatives approved the Cyber Security Enhancement Act. Now if a cyber crime results in the death of an individual, the offender could face a life sentence. There has been additional fall-out from the September 11th attacks with the FBI and other government security agencies dramatically escalating their monitoring of the Internet. This has pushed some hackers further underground, fearful that what they had previously been doing out of boredom or challenge could now be viewed as an act of terrorism.

F. On the other hand, the events of September 11th have led to some ex-hackers using their extensive knowledge and experience to join forces with security forces to aid the fight against terrorism.

G. However, even with the increased threats of punishment, computer viruses and incidents of hacking continue to be widespread. Long-time security measures which have been utilised by companies and individuals are not fail-safe. One of the more prevalent IS security measures is the use of firewalls, which 'filter' the data entering/ leaving the corporate IS. It is true that these firewalls have a number of advantages, nevertheless, they should not be seen as a panacea to all IS security woes, merely an enhancement. They can provide a false sense of security and have limited protection from internal attackers. In short, the corporate world needs to realise that computer security will be an on-going problem <u>and</u> expense.

Questions 1 - 3

Complete the table below with information found in the text.
*Use **NO MORE THAN THREE WORDS OR A NUMBER** for each answer. Write your answers in boxes 1 - 3 on your Answer Sheet.*

Date	Event
1996	commercial sector constituted **(1)** .... of Internet usage.
(2)	Computer Emergency Response Team formed
Post-September 11th 2001	FBI increased **(3)** ....

Questions 4 - 9

*In Reading Passage 1 there are several sections. Choose the most suitable heading (**I – IX**) from the box below which best matches the Sections **A - G**. Write your answers in boxes 4 - 9 on your Answer Sheet.*

NOTE: *there are more headings than sections so you will not use all of them. You may use any of the headings more than once.*

LIST OF HEADINGS
I   A positive aspect of hacking
II   Tougher punishments for hackers
III   Response to Internet security
IV   Growth of the Internet
V   Responsibilities of managers
VI   Hackers v administrators
VII Difficulty of detection
VIII Government agencies
IX Common security measure

		Answer
Example:	Paragraph A	.....**IV**......

4	Paragraph B	....		7	Paragraph E	....
5	Paragraph C	....		8	Paragraph F	....
6	Paragraph D	....		9	Paragraph G	....

Questions 10 - 13

Complete the sentences below.
Use **NO MORE THAN THREE WORDS** for each answer. Write your answers in boxes 10 - 13 on your
Answer Sheet.

10 Solving the Morris worm was difficult because the repair method was sent

.... and therefore useless.

11 The teenager who hacked into Bell Atlantic would get a maximum prison sentence of

.... if he committed the same crime now.

12 Some hackers are scared that government authorities could now consider them to be

....

13 One disadvantage of .... is that they can make a company
feel protected from attack even though the system is not perfect.

READING PASSAGE 2

Questions 14 - 27 are based on Reading Passage 2.

THE BIG SLEEP

The nature of sleep and the role it plays in our lives has long fascinated science and been the focus of
many studies and a great deal of research.

A. The benefit of receiving enough sleep is essential to our inner well-being. Not enough sleep, however,
means that we lack the opportunity to restore ourselves physiologically, emotionally and cognitively. It
affects our mood and can result in behaviour and performance problems. When we sleep, our bodies
rest but our brains are active. Sleep lays the groundwork for a productive day ahead. Although most
people benefit the most from eight hours of sleep each night, this is not always what they manage to
achieve. Men get slightly less sleep than women during the week (6.7 hours/night vs. 7.0 hours/night),
but have fewer sleep problems, according to recent Sleep in America polls conducted annually by the
National Sleep Foundation (NSF).

B. According to current scientific thought, the human body is pre-programmed for sleep. At nightfall,
cells in the retina (a light sensitive membrane connected to the eye by the optic nerve) send a sleep
signal to a cluster of nerve cells in the brain. These nerve cells are concentrated together in the
suprachiasmatic nucleus (SCN) and are located in a part of the brain called the hypothalamus which
helps regulate body temperature. The SCN is also known as the circadian clock. This biological clock
relays the message to other parts of the brain which then signals the body that it is time to sleep. For
instance, the pineal gland, also located in the hypothalamus, produces a substance called melatonin,
which lowers body temperature, and causes drowsiness.

C. A great deal of the information we now know about sleep and the physiological changes it causes in
the brain can be traced back to the invention of the electroencephalogram in the 1950s. This machine
allowed scientists to record the feeble electric currents generated on the brain without opening the skull
and to depict them graphically onto a strip of paper. Brain-wave function could be examined and scientists
could thereby observe sleep from moment to moment. In the 1970s it became possible for scientists to
make assumptions about the role that correct breathing plays during sleep with the development of the
technology to measure respiration. It was here that science really began to understand the nature of
sleep and the role it plays in people s lives.

D. As well as uncovering the physiological changes occurring during sleep, <u>The New England Journal of Medicine</u> reported that sleep concerns were a public health threat as serious as smoking and in the years since, medical researchers have linked sleep disorders with many life-threatening diseases. Even though more than 70 million Americans have a sleeping problem, most cases go undiagnosed and untreated, so the true economic and sociological damage caused by these disorders is unknown although, the economic cost is conservatively estimated to be billions of dollars a year in healthcare costs and lost productivity. Breathing problems during sleep represent by far the greatest proportion of sleep disorders and cause the most concern, with studies showing that between 50% and 80% of stroke and heart failure patients have breathing problems during sleep.

E. Scientific studies have found that children who are identified as snorers or those who have poor sleeping patterns at around the age of four or five, scored lower than average in Intelligence Quotient (IQ) tests, not only during the sleep deprivation period but subsequent to that. There are also suggestions that ongoing sleep deprivation in adults can cause permanent damage.

F. Teenagers can have peculiar sleep requirements. It has always been known that adolescents spend more time sleeping than adults, but science has only recently isolated the reasons for this. Research now shows that growth hormones are secreted during slow-wave sleep and teenagers do indeed, need more of this kind of sleep than at any other stage in their lives. Chronic lack of sleep among teenagers means that as a group they are more likely to use stimulants and experience negative mood swings. Statistics also indicate that young drivers are responsible for more than one-half of fall-asleep crashes.

G. However, it is not just young people who pay the price for lack of proper sleep. Workers are robbing themselves of sleep in order to increase productivity in both their social and working lives. In recent years, however, the identification of driver fatigue as the possible cause of 1/3 of all accidents provides some indication of the price we are paying for such a trade-off. Extensive scientific research indicates that chronic tiredness has been the cause of environmental disasters, nuclear mishaps and several well-documented near misses in the air. Scientists are beginning to argue that the lengthening of the working day is harming workers, their families and society. In the long run, productivity will suffer.

H. As a reaction against this disturbing trend, there has been increased support for regulation of the number of hours worked by employees in demanding jobs, such as doctors, nurses, pilots, bus drivers and truck drivers. Legislation is being drafted to limit work hours, thus forcing companies to become instrumental in changing work cultures to ensure employees are getting enough rest and leisure time in order to avoid chronic tiredness and its devastating consequences.

Questions 14 – 16

*Choose the correct letter from (**A – D**) and write it in boxes 14 - 16 on your answer sheet.*

14   The SCN

    A   is regulated by the hypothalamus.
    B   is affected by fading light.
    C   is located in the brain.
    D   tells the body it is time for sleep.

15   Scientists' involvement with sleep research

    A   is driven by the potential of monetary gains to be made.
    B   is a recent trend.
    C   has been advanced with technological developments.
    D   has relied on observations and assumptions about sleep being made.

16   Sleeping disorders are

    A   linked to fatal diseases and conditions.
    B   one of the main causes of strokes and heart failure.
    C   common in babies.
    D   unusual but can be life-threatening.

Questions 17– 19

Look at the following statements (Questions 17 - 19). Indicate:

TRUE   *if the statement agrees with information in the passage*
FALSE   *if the statement contradicts information in the passage*
NOT GIVEN   *if the information is not given in the passage*

Write your answers in boxes 17 - 19 on your Answer Sheet.

		Answer
Example:	80% of all stroke patients experience breathing problems in their sleep.	**FALSE**

17   Sleep deprivation can affect intellectual performance in adults.   ....

18   Longer working hours have resulted in productivity increases.   ....

19   Companies have to be more active in preventing accidents caused by
     human factors.   ....

Questions 20 - 27

*Choose the statement (**I - X**) below that best summarises each paragraph (**A - H**) in Reading Passage 2. Write your answers in boxes 20 – 27 on your Answer Sheet.*

NOTE: *there are more statements than paragraphs so you will not use them all.*

20	Paragraph A	....	24	Paragraph E	....
21	Paragraph B	....	25	Paragraph F	....
22	Paragraph C	....	26	Paragraph G	....
23	Paragraph D	....	27	Paragraph H	....

LIST OF SUMMARY STATEMENTS

I   The negative effects of chronic sleep deprivation have tragic consequences.

II   There are many advantages to getting sufficient sleep.

III   Current medical research maintains that sleep is critical to early development.

IV   Technological advances contributed significantly to sleep research.

V   Efforts are being made to decrease the incidence of work-related accidents
          and disasters.

VI   Sleep problems affect a significant percentage of the population and have
          far-reaching consequences.

VII   Lack of the right kind of sleep can affect behaviour.

VIII   Physiological changes occur to create sleep.

IX   Sleep has an important function in our daily lives.

X   The electroencephalogram revolutionised sleep research.

READING PASSAGE 3

Questions 28 - 40 are based on Reading Passage 3.

SALINISATION

Salinisation (the accumulation of salts in soil) is one of today's worst environmental disasters and yet it does not share the global spotlight with other ecological issues. Considering the threat that salinisation poses to nearly all irrigated drylands and the consequential impact on traditional agriculture, such lagging public awareness is, at the very least, disconcerting. Reports indicate that between 2.5 and 6 million hectares of land are affected by salinisation and unless precautionary and remedial measures are implemented, economic and environmental repercussions will be inevitable.

Contributing ecological factors such as soil-type, climate, rainfall and topography make some lands more vulnerable to the salinisation process. However, the vast majority of land degraded through salinisation can be directly linked to human activity, whether it be destroying natural vegetation and bushlands to clear the land for farms, over-irrigation of cultivated land and/or poor farming practices. Countries like Australia are beginning to see the devastation of increasing salinity levels after a relatively short period of introduced European farming methods.

Salts such as sodium chloride and calcium sulphates, occur naturally in many soils and waterways. When the concentration of salt levels (salinity) in soil becomes too high, plant growth is adversely affected and the soil structure can be damaged.

Nature dealt reasonably successfully with salinity levels in Australia prior to European settlement. Natural vegetation, including perennial grasses and deep-rooted trees, ensured that salts were dissolved as rainwater slowly filtered down through the soil. Salt was moved downward and remained in the groundwater below the root zone of the plants. The fibrous root structure of those native plants, acted as an effective filter with their high water-holding capacity. Some rainwater was held by the roots and some rainwater leached downwards through the soil carrying the dissolved salts. Groundwater transpired back into the air through the foliage of the native plants.

As Europeans introduced traditional forms of agriculture and cleared large areas of land for grazing in the 1800s, much of the native vegetation in Australia was replaced by generally shallow-rooted annual crops and pastures, substantially changing the natural process that had been working well. These crops and pastures use less water than original native vegetation and the roots do not have the same water-holding capacity. With the introduction of these crops, more rainwater and irrigated water makes its way downwards through the soil to below the root-zone. The water still carries the dissolved salts downwards past the root-zone but the amount and level of groundwater is increased. In addition, because the roots of these crops do not hold as much water, the water is drawn back up from the groundwater later, as the plant needs moisture.

We see then that the amount and level of groundwater increases because of an increase in the amount of water being put into the soil and not being held in fibrous root structures like that of native vegetation. This causes the water table to rise bringing dissolved salts with it that eventually reach the surface of the soil. Water is then evaporated from the surface leaving high concentrations of salts behind. This is the process of salinisation.

Soils with high salinity levels occur naturally in Australia but these were mostly confined to particular coastal and sub-coastal areas. Over the past 200 years, the total area affected by salinisation has expanded and has now spread to inland areas. Groundwater salts that have been accumulating over thousands of years are now rising to the surface. When this groundwater enters the root zone of the cultivated plants which are naturally not salt tolerant, the plants die. The effects are not limited to the particular cleared site where soil becomes unsuitable for plant production. Salty groundwater can travel along the natural contours of the land into other agricultural areas, creating salty discharge sites quite some distance from the recharge zone. Native aquatic and land-based habitats are now at risk, threatening the biological diversity in Australia. It is therefore necessary for groundwater and surface run-off water to be dealt with.

Land managers or farmers do not have to wait until crops die to recognize that salinity levels are out of control. Declining yields in crop production, sick or dying trees around the property or the appearance of salt-tolerant species all serve as a warning that salinity levels have increased. If these signs are ignored and the lands become degraded, combating salinity will become expensive and time-consuming.

One current practice is to replant trees in an effort to draw the water table down and slow the salinisation process but this alone will be inadequate. Investigations are also being made into planting salt-tolerant crops and pastures whilst building up and preserving native species and remnant bushland areas. More effective techniques to counteract the drainage problems in the form of drainage canals are also being canvassed. These hope to achieve a balance between the volume of water entering the soil in the recharge zone and the volume of water that leaves as discharge.

The key to fighting salinity is through long-term management practices on agricultural land that recognize the importance of the role that native vegetation plays in keeping water balance in the soil. These practices will need to consider agricultural requirements along with land and water care i.e. balancing economic development with environmental protection. Moreover, a public awareness campaign with government-funded incentives must make it clear that current farming practices in at-risk landscapes are not sustainable and cannot be tolerated.

GLOSSARY

salinisation	- the build-up of concentrations of salt levels within the soil
groundwater	- water that is held in the soil
water table	- the level of groundwater
transpiration	- the loss of water through the leaves of plants

Questions 28 – 35

Complete the summary below. Choose words and phrases from the box below the summary and write your answers in boxes 28 – 35 on your Answer Sheet. Use each word or phrase ONCE only.

Many people are unaware of the **(28)** .... to land that salinity is causing in countries like

Australia. Salinity has many causes, including **(29)** .... and short-sighted farming strategies

like over-irrigation. Even though salts are present in many soils and waterways, native plants

(30) .... to ensure that salt remained in the groundwater, under the root zones. Introduced or

exotic species of plants with their different needs and plant structure, allow more **(31)** ....

into the soil, causing the **(32)** .... to rise. Because salts cannot be evaporated, as they rise

with the groundwater and reach the **(33)** .... , the high level of salts cause salinisation. The

resultant rising salt levels can have detrimental effects on all biological groups not only at the

(34) .... If we do not take note of the **(35)** .... , the costs involved in repairing the

salt damage will be considerable.

land clearing	recharge zone	warning signs
had evaporated	salinity level	European
had recharged	trees	had adapted
water table	surface	farming difficulties
habitats	government	water
rainwater	degradation	air

Questions 36 – 40

Look at the following statements (Questions 36 - 40). Indicate:

YES	*if the statement agrees with information in the passage*
NO	*if the statement contradicts information in the passage*
NOT GIVEN	*if the information is not given in the passage*

Write your answers in boxes 36 - 40 on your Answer Sheet.

Answer

36   If non-native crops held more water in their roots, the level of
groundwater would not increase.   ....

37   Coastal land is now less habitable as a result of salinisation.   ....

38   Where the water table has risen, groundwater may seep into the soil
surface at discharge areas.   ....

39   Re-planting native vegetation would stop the water table rising and
eliminate salts in soils.   ....

40   All of the suggested remediation practices in the passage aim to re-balance
the amount of water in the soil.   ....

PRACTICE TEST 3 - WRITING

WRITING TASK 1

You should spend about 20 minutes on this task.

> *The pie graphs below show the results of a survey of children's activities. The first graph shows the cultural and leisure activities that boys participate in, whereas the second graph shows the activities in which girls participate.*

> *Write a report describing the information shown in the two pie graphs.*

You should write at least 150 words.

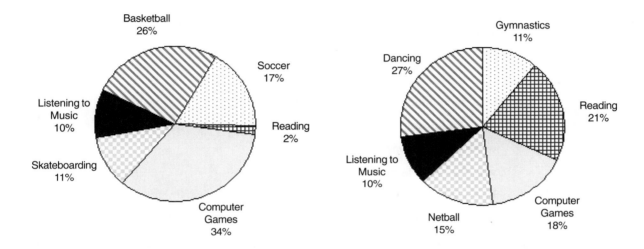

WRITING TASK 2

You should spend about 40 minutes on this task.

Present a written argument to an educated reader with no specialist knowledge on the following topic:

> *Discuss the advantages and disadvantages of living and working in a foreign country.*

You should use your own ideas, knowledge and experience and support your arguments with examples and relevant evidence.

You should write at least 250 words.

PRACTICE TEST 3 - SPEAKING

► **PART 1:** (4 – 5 minutes) Introduction and (getting to know you) interview

Examiner: *Good morning. My name's ....*
And your name is...? And you're from... ?
Can I see your passport please? Thank you.

- *Who do you live with in ..... ?*
- *Can you describe your room to me?*
- *What do you do to relax in the evenings?*
- *Do you like playing sport?*
- *Do you enjoy studying English?*
- *Can you remember your first English lesson?*
- *What do you plan to do after this speaking test?*

Thank you.

► **PART 2:** (3 – 4 minutes) Individual long turn (monologue)

Examiner: *Now I'm going to give you a card with some information about* **SPORTING EVENTS***.*
You will have one minute to read the card and then I'd like you to talk about **SPORTING**
EVENTS *for one or two minutes. You can make some notes to help you wish. All right?*

Describe a memorable sporting event that you participated in or watched.

You should say:

what the event was

why the event is memorable

how you felt at the event

...and describe whether or not winning or losing is a significant memory.

Examiner: *Would you like to start now?*

You give your talk and after 1 or 2 minutes the examiner will ask you a question or two.

- *Do you often go to sporting events?*
- *Are you very competitive?*

Thank you.

► **PART 3:** (4 – 5 minutes) Two way discussion (more abstract conversation)

Examiner: *Now I'd like to ask you a few more questions.*

- *Governments allocate large amounts of money to sporting events such as the Olympics. Do you agree with this spending?*
- *Can or should sport play a significant role in developing international relations?*
- *The idea of sportsmanship has changed over the years. Should professional sports-players act in a particular way?*
- *A significant amount of money and time is spent on testing for the use of drugs in sport. How important is this?*
- *Large companies now sponsor major sporting events and teams. Can this sponsorship lead to problems?*
- *What do you think the future of international sports will be?*

Thank you very much.
That's the end of the speaking test. Goodbye.

PRACTICE TEST 4 - LISTENING

SECTION 1:   QUESTIONS 1 – 10

Listen to two students talking about libraries in Australia.

Questions 1 – 2

*Choose the correct letter from **A** - **D** for each answer.*

Example: Why is Yumi worried?

    A She's a new student.
    B She doesn't know very much about libraries.
    C She hasn't used a library much.
    D She has a lot of assignments.

    ANSWER: **B**

---

1   Who advised Yumi to join the local library?

    A her flatmate
    B Mary Ann
    C the librarian
    D Mary Ann and Yumi's flatmate

2   What items cannot be borrowed from the local library?

    A   **B**   **C**   **D**

Questions 3 – 4

*Choose the correct answers from **A** - **C** for each answer.*

3   If Yumi returns a book two days after the loan period has ended,

    A she will have to pay a fine.
    B she will have to pay 10 cents.
    C it won't cost her anything.

4   Why hasn't Yumi been to the university library yet?

    A She couldn't attend the orientation activities.
    B She has been sick all week.
    C She had to go to her lecture.

Questions 5 – 9

Label the map of the library below.
Choose the correct letter from **A – E**
for each answer.

5   Returns Box   ....

6   Library Computers   ....

7   Monograph Collection   ....

8   Reference Section   ....

9   Advisors' Desk   ....

Question 10

Complete the sentence below.
Use **NO MORE THAN THREE WORDS** for your answer.

10   Yumi should borrow Recommended Texts from the library as soon as possible

because ....

SECTION 2:   QUESTIONS 11 – 20

Questions 11 - 16

Complete the notes below.
Use **NO MORE THAN THREE WORDS OR A NUMBER** for each answer.

INTERNATIONAL DRIVING LICENSES

FACTS:
- have been used **(11)** ....
- drivers do not have to speak the native tongue of the country they are visiting
- drivers must be at least 18 years of age
- drivers must hold a driving license in their home country

SPECIFICATIONS OF BOOKLET:

Size of license: 10.8 x **(12)** .... cms

Number of pages: 17

Colour of inside pages: **(13)** ....

Has a photograph of the driver and their **(14)** ....

Available from authorized travel agencies and the **(15)** ....

Cost of 3 year license: **(16)** ....

Questions 17 – 20

Complete the summary of International Driving Licenses below.
Use **NO MORE THAN THREE WORDS** *for each answer.*

International Driving Licenses cannot be used in the **(17)** .... They may only be used in

some countries for **(18)** .... Drivers using International Driving Licenses must obey the **(19)**

.... of the country that they are driving in. The driver must be responsible for learning

the rules of the host country, because if they break the rules, they may be **(20)** ....

SECTION 3: QUESTIONS 21 – 30

Questions 21 – 24

Complete the chart below.
*Match the advantages of joining a learning circle (**I – VI**) to the person.*

NOTE: *there are more advantages listed than you will need.*

Reasons for joining a learning circle given by:	
Economics tutor	**(21)** ....
Hamish	**(22)** ....
	(23) ....
Anita	**(24)** ....

Advantages of a learning circle

> I   commits to other students with a shared purpose
>
> II   can provide motivation to study
>
> III   commits time to study
>
> IV   can provide help with understanding subject material
>
> V   can provide support for other students
>
> VI   saves the cost of an expensive tutor

Questions 25 – 27

*Choose the correct letter from **A - C** for each answer.*

25   The purpose of studying past exam papers is to

    A   do well in the end of term exam.
    B   contribute to the learning circle.
    C   compare answers of past papers with other students.

26   By doing mock tutorials in the learning circle, the students hope to

    A   practise by themselves first.
    B   help each other by giving practical advice.
    C   gain self-confidence.

27   Hamish advises Anita to

    A   make a list of objectives for the first learning circle.
    B   commit to the learning circle and then get a tutor.
    C   trial the learning circle first.

Question 28

*Choose the correct letter from **A - D**.*

28   When was/is the first learning circle study session?

    A   last week
    B   next week
    C   thursday, 6th August
    D   this evening

Questions 29 - 30

*Choose **TWO** letters from **A - E**.*

29 & 30   Which two activities are most likely to be discussed at the next learning circle?

    A   past exam papers
    B   learning styles
    C   lecture notes
    D   reading comprehension
    E   how to re-write lecture notes

SECTION 4:   QUESTIONS 31 – 40

Questions 31 - 32

Complete the notes below.
*Use **NO MORE THAN THREE WORDS** for each answer.*

Reasons given for speaker adopting wind-generating power:

- lives on a windy farm
- electricity not supplied by (31) ....
- diesel and petrol generators' lack of efficiency and excessive (32) ....

Questions 33 - 36

Complete the time-line below.
*Use **NO MORE THAN THREE WORDS OR A NUMBER** for each answer.*

1975	-	speaker bought farm
	-	relied on diesel and petrol generators
Late 1975	-	Hybrid system installed
	-	Successful even in **(33)** ....
(34)	-	stopped operating **(35)** .... and relied solely on wind generator
	-	imported four wind generators from the **(36)** .... who now supply 50% of world's wind turbines
Last year	-	bought 600-kilowatt wind turbine

Questions 37 - 39

Look at the picture of wind turbines below and complete the following information.

Details of a 600-kilowatt wind turbine given by the speaker	
(37)	46 metres
Diameter of rotors:	43.5 metres
Power output:	**(38)** .... kilowatt hours per year
Life expectancy:	20 years
Maintenance:	**(39)** .... a year

Question 40

Complete the sentence below.
*Use **NO MORE THAN THREE WORDS** for your answer.*

40 Possible sources of future income for the speaker include:

- tourists visiting the 'wind farm'.
- .... to State Electricity Commission.

PRACTICE TEST 4 - READING

READING PASSAGE 1

Questions 1 - 13 are based on *Reading Passage 1*.

 ## HOME – THE NEW WORKPLACE

One of the scourges of the modern world is the length of time we take commuting to and from work. In large cities this can mean losing three or more hours every day just traveling from home to work and back again. Surely there is an alternative! Well, according to a survey conducted in the US, 22% of people would much prefer working from home, should circumstances allow. Liz Sewell spoke to several people who have already made the change to this modern-day workplace to try and find out more.

Scott Miller is a 40-year-old draughtsman who has been working from home for the past two years. He admits that it wasn't something that he craved for; rather it happened when his wife, Jules, a university lecturer, was offered a full-time position. "She didn't think that she could take the job. I knew that she really wanted it, but she didn't want to put our son into full-time care. I had been working for the same firm for seven years and decided to approach my bosses. My track record probably helped because they accepted the proposition. As long as my productivity was maintained, they didn't mind where I worked. Also my wife is happy, and her career is blossoming."

"Now I go into the office every Monday afternoon for a meeting and to pick up my week's work. Interestingly, I feel that I work even better from home, so much so that even though our son is now at school, I still work there."

However, is working from home as simple as it sounds? Transferring work to a different workplace is only part of the equation for Joanne McCarthy, who until three months ago was a Human Resources Manager for a large public corporation. She has now become a full-time trader on the stock market. She says she loves the freedom that working from home gives her, but she really misses the social interaction.

"As my job just involves working for myself, by myself, I find that I have become much more introverted because I don't have that face-to-face, professional involvement with people any more. I spend all day on the computer checking the prices of my stocks. By evening, I am desperate to talk to my husband – even if it is only about what he has been doing all day".

She has realized that this could jeopardise her attempts to work from home and has decided to join a local investors' club which meets once a week, just to get more interaction in her life. "'I don't think I'll learn anything from it, but it will be nice to meet with like-minded people and talk business. Meeting friends for coffee or for lunch meets my social needs, but work is still a large part of my life."

One of Joanne's friends helped her to make the transition to working from home. Louise Tate is an accountant and used to commute an hour each way to her office before deciding there had to be a better way. For her, the biggest problem with working from home was distractions. "It was so easy to get distracted by the other things you have to do at home, like washing and cleaning," she told us. "I had to force myself to view my study as an office, not part of the house. So I came up with a novel idea - my husband thought I was mad, but I had a separate entrance built to the office. At the beginning of my workday, I go out of the front door of our house, lock it, and then walk around to the office. Now I feel that I am really at work, and my productivity has increased as a result. I know it sounds strange, but it works for me." Twelve months down the track and Louise never wants to face the morning traffic again.

People choose to work from home for a multitude of reasons. Take the example of George Mercer, who owns seven cafés within a 7 mile radius of downtown Miami. He has based his office in his Fort Lauderdale beachfront home, and keeps in contact with his various managers by phone, fax and email. "When I started the business four years ago, I couldn't decide which café to have as my main base, so I decided to set up my office at home. With modern telecommunications nowadays, I am always able to contact my premises and order provisions from my suppliers."

"If I get fed up with working from home, or if there are problems that have to be dealt with in person, I just jump in the car and drive to the cafes. From time to time, we have meetings at my place, which give the managers a break from their own 'offices'. They get a change of scenery. I still have control but they have a large amount of independence in the day-to-day running of the cafés. I love my job and it's obvious that my managers respond well to the arrangement. Life's great at the moment and I wouldn't change a thing!"

Obviously, not everyone is able to have the type of work that can be done from home, but there are plenty of people just like me – judging by internet sites and the more traditional employment vacancy ads - who would jump at the chance.

Questions 1 – 8

*Using information from Reading Passage 1, match the people listed (**A – F**) in the box below with their descriptions (**Questions 1 – 8**). Write the answers in boxes 1 – 8 on your Answer Sheet.*

NOTE: *there are more descriptions than people. You may use any of the choices more than once.*

A	Scott Miller
B	Joanne McCarthy
C	Louise Tate
D	George Mercer
E	None of the above
F	All of the above

1 .... needs to be good at maths.

2 .... is not self-employed.

3 .... has been working from home for the longest period.

4 .... altered their house to be able to work at home.

5 .... doesn't need to interact with clients to carry out their business.

6 .... thinks that they are less successful working from home.

7 .... helped someone else to retain his/her career.

8 .... lives on the coast.

Questions 9 – 13

*Choose the correct letter from **A - D** for each answer and write it in boxes 9 – 13 on your Answer Sheet.*

9   Scott Miller

   A   had always wanted to work from home.
   B   no longer has the original reason for working from home.
   C   had difficulty persuading his employer to let him do it.
   D   only visits the office for staff meetings.

10   Joanne McCarthy

   A   sometimes has regrets about working from home.
   B   enjoys talking about her work with her husband.
   C   is still learning her business.
   D   is determined to ensure that working from home satisfies her.

11   Louise Tate

    A got angry with her husband about the office door.

    B had to have a total change of mindset to be able to work from home.

    C often gets distracted by her domestic duties.

    D recommends working from home.

12   George Mercer

    A does all his business using modern telecommunications.

    B usually only sees his managers at scheduled meetings.

    C lives less than 7 miles from any of his cafés.

    D None of the above.

13   The writer of this article

    A is envious of these people being able to work from home.

    B works from home herself.

    C doesn't give her opinion on the subject.

    D plans to work from home in the future.

READING PASSAGE 2

Questions 14 - 27 are based on Reading Passage 2.

ALZHEIMER'S DISEASE
ALZHEIMER'S DISEASE ALZHEIMER'S

Alzheimer's disease is a progressive, neurodegenerative disease which is caused by physiological changes to the brain. It changes the delicate organisation of the nerve cells in the brain by creating the gradual spread of sticky plaques and clumps of tangled fibres. As brain cells stop communicating with each other, they atrophy, causing memory and reasoning to fade. Tangles and plaques first appear in the entorhinal cortex, an essential memory-processing centre needed for creating memories and retrieving old ones. This does not affect detailed complex memories, but rather the simple recollections of facts that allow us to function socially, such as birthdays and lunch dates. Over time they move higher, invading the hippocampus, that part of the brain that forms complex memories of events or objects. These kinds of memories are, of necessity, more detailed and involve longer recollections. It allows us to recall how to function at work and complete reasonably complex tasks but without the need to analyse or make judgements. Finally, the tangles and plaques reach the top of the brain or the neocortex, the executive that sorts through stimuli and orchestrates behaviour. Here, amongst other functions, we are using analytical skills to evaluate, digest and respond to situations appropriately.

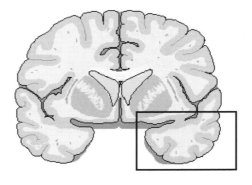

Area of the brain where Alzheimer's is believed to begin

The onset of the disease is characterised by an initial memory decline and, over several years, it destroys cognition, personality and the ability to function, but preserves motor function. Confusion and restlessness may also occur. It is a progressive disease and the type, severity, sequence and progression of any mental changes that occur vary widely. The early symptoms of Alzheimer's which include forgetfulness and loss of concentration, can easily be missed because they resemble the natural signs of aging. Similar symptoms can also result from fatigue, grief, depression, illness, vision or hearing loss, the use of alcohol or certain medications, or simply the burden of too many details to remember at once. A cure is not imminent, there is no way to deter the progression of the disease and its precise cause is largely mysterious. On average, 10% of people over 65 will contract Alzheimer's disease, a number that rises to 50% by the age of 80. Its onset may occur as early as the age of 40. Approximately 100,000 victims die and 360,000 new cases of Alzheimer's disease are diagnosed each year. It is estimated that by the year 2050, 14 million Americans will have this disease.

Much current knowledge about this illness comes from a single piece of ongoing research: The Nun Study. Since 1986, David Snowdon, a scientist from the University of Kentucky, has been studying 678 School Sisters. To Snowdon, this group of elderly women represented an ideal population for studying the disease: their economic status, health care and living conditions are uniform with fewer variations in lifestyle to confound the data. Of course, the very homogeneity of this population means Snowdon's study has its detractors – for example, the nuns face few of the stresses of modern life, nor do they smoke or drink. Some of the factors that lead to Alzheimer's disease may not be present in their lives. But whatever the limits, Dr Snowdon's study has achieved a 68% compliance rate among the sisters in that religious community, and continues after death with post-mortem examinations of their brains, and thus promising much valuable information. Over the years, Snowdon and his colleagues have discovered a series of unexpected links between lifestyle and Alzheimer's disease. It has been known for some time that genes can predispose people to Alzheimer's disease, but Snowdon's study has shown that other factors play an important part in the development of this dreadful disease.

Some of the results of the study have been widely publicised. The study found that those nuns whose early autobiographies contained complex grammar and a greater density of ideas had the lowest risk of developing Alzheimer's disease. This result that isolates complexity in writing as a protector against Alzheimer's disease suggests a correlation between higher brain capacity and lowered risk. Preliminary studies also seemed to indicate that those nuns whose early autobiographies suggested a predisposition to negative emotions had a higher risk of Alzheimer's disease than those who were more optimistic in the way they conveyed their written ideas. Other important findings of the study include the fact that stroke increases the risk of Alzheimer's disease. Evidence of stroke, including those undiagnosed before death, as well as earlier brain trauma, as from head injury, was more prevalent in those nuns who died of Alzheimer's Disease than in those who died without that diagnosis. Dr Snowdon's research also confirms the suspicion that folate deficiency might contribute to Alzheimer's disease. High folate levels appear to have been protective in these nuns. This ties in with other studies which have shown that folic acid deficiency plays a role in some forms of mental retardation in children and in some cognitive problems in adults.

New research is showing that the decline in cognitive function may start sooner than previously thought. Scientists suggest that a condition known as mild cognitive impairment, in which patients in their forties and fifties exhibit memory and recall problems, is very likely the first step along the way to Alzheimer's disease. If so, then it is important to start slowdown strategies as soon as possible.

> **Glossary:**
>
> The *entorhinal cortex*, the *hippocampus* and the *neocortex* are those parts of the brain that are primarily affected by Alzheimer's disease.
>
> plaque – fibre-like substance which multiplies in the brain of Alzheimer's sufferers.
>
> folate – is water-soluble vitamin B occurring naturally in foods such as leafy green vegetables, some fortified cereals and grain products.

Questions 14 – 17

*Using information from Reading Passage 2 match the physiological causes (**A – C**) in the box below with the effects on memory (**Questions 14 - 17**). Write the answers in boxes 14 - 17 on your Answer Sheet.*

PHYSIOLOGICAL CAUSES

A tangles and plaques in the entorhinal cortex

B tangles and plaques in the hippocampus

C tangles and plaques in the neocortex

---

14 .... difficulty recalling what you ate for breakfast this morning

15 .... difficulty completing a detailed work related report

16 .... difficulty remembering someone's name

17 .... difficulty in using the photocopying machine at work

Questions 18 - 24

Complete the summary by using words and phrases from the list provided in the box below. Write your answers in boxes 18 - 24 on your Answer Sheet.

NOTE: *there are more words than you need and you may use any word or phrase more than once.*

functions	victims	genetic predisposition	limited
future	examined	unexpected links	absent
slowed	short term	been indicating	movement
decreased	gets smaller	characteristics	discovered

Alzheimer's disease is an illness that robs its victims of memory, personality and finally all cognitive function. It does not affect **(18)** .... It is impossible to predict how the disease will progress because its **(19)** .... vary greatly. Diagnosis in the early stages is difficult because symptoms resemble the consequences of normal aging and can also be the result of a number of other unrelated ailments. There is no hope for a cure in the **(20)** .... and once someone has the disease, its progression cannot be **(21)** .... The percentage of people contracting Alzheimer's disease increases with age. Ongoing research has been conducted in the form of The Nun Study which has **(22)** .... the physiological changes and lifestyles of 678 nuns in America from 1986. The study has been criticised because some of the factors that may lead to Alzheimer's disease were **(23)** .... in the nuns' lives. Nonetheless the study provides invaluable data. The study has isolated connections between lifestyle and Alzheimer's disease that occur independently of **(24)** ....

Questions 25 - 26

*Complete the information below by identifying **TWO** other indicators that protect from Alzheimer's disease. Use **NO MORE THAN THREE WORDS** from Reading Passage 2 for each answer.*

> **The Nun Study**
>
> **Indicators that protect from Alzheimer's disease:**
>
> - higher complexity in writing
>
> - (25) ....
>
> - no history of head trauma or stroke
>
> - (26) ....

READING PASSAGE 3

Questions 27 - 40 are based on Reading Passage 3.

GLOBALI$ATION

For many, the surprise of finding a McDonalds outlet in Moscow or Beijing provides no greater symbol of the spread of globalisation. Used to explain all manner of economic, cultural and political change that has swept over the world in recent decades, globalisation is a term that continues to cause intellectual debate. Some see it as inevitable and desirable, but it is a contentious issue with an increasing number of individual citizens around the world questioning whether or not the implications of globalization, in terms of international distribution of income and decreasing poverty, are effective.

The beginning of globalisation is inextricably linked to technological improvements in the field of international communications and a fall in the cost of international transport and travel. Entrepreneurs and power-brokers took advantage of these advances to invest capital into foreign countries. This became the basic mechanism for globalisation with the trading of currencies, stocks and bonds growing rapidly.

Breaking down the barriers through the free movement of capital, free trade and political co-operation was seen as a positive move that would not only increase living standards around the world, but also raise political and environmental awareness, especially in developing countries. Predictions were that nations would become more outward-looking in their policy-making, as they searched for opportunities to increase economic growth. Roles would be assigned to various players around the globe as capital providers, exporters of technology, suppliers of services, sources of labour, etc. Consequently, countries and economies could concentrate on what they were good at and as a result, markets would experience increased efficiency.

The process of economic globalisation was without doubt led by commercial and financial power-brokers but there were many others who supported the integration of world economies. As multinational companies searched for new work-forces and raw materials, non-government organizations and lobby groups were optimistic that in the wake of global business, indigenous cultures might be given a reprieve with an injection of foreign capital. This would, in turn, provide local employment opportunities. By spreading trade more evenly between developed and developing nations, it was touted that poverty would decrease and living standards would rise.

Governments saw the chance to attract multinational companies with tax-breaks and incentives to set up in-country, effectively buying employment opportunities for their constituents.

By the late 1990s, some trepidation started to surface and globalisation faced its most public setback. The spectacular economic collapses in Korea, Brazil, Thailand and other countries were considered, rightly or wrongly, to be caused by the outwardly-oriented trade policies that globalisation espoused such as the growth of exports. These countries had enjoyed record growth for a relatively short time, but when faced with difficulties, the growth appeared unsustainable. The vulnerability and risk associated with reliance on exports and international markets was made clear.

Meanwhile though, through the 1990s and early 2000s, multinational companies continued to do well financially. Profits were increasing, keeping shareholders happy, but the anticipated spin-offs were not being felt at the workers' level or in local communities in the form of increased employment. These successful companies did not want to share the benefits of the increased efficiency they were receiving as a result of introducing their own work practices. The multinationals were setting their own agendas, with governments, in many cases, turning a blind eye fearing that they might pull out and cause more unemployment. Free trade was now accused of restricting governments, who were no longer setting the rules, and domestic markets felt increasingly threatened by the power that the multinationals had.

The negative consequences of globalisation have now become a concern for many protest groups in different nations. If the concept of globalisation was meant to benefit all nations, they say, then it has failed. Rich countries, like America, continue to grow richer and more powerful with many of the head offices of multinationals based there. The economies of some developing countries though, especially in Africa, are making only negligible if any progress in the war against poverty. As a result, protestors are confronting the advocates of globalisation on their own doorstep as power-players meet at economic summits in already-globalised cities.

The International Monetary Fund (IMF) maintains that globalisation has succeeded in establishing a more equitable share of world-trade and remains optimistic that the gulf between rich and poorer nations, given the right conditions, will be considerably lessened in the future. They point out that no country can afford to opt out of globalisation and, indeed, would be foolish to attempt to do so. They maintain that 'non-globalising developing countries' have made slower progress than 'globalising developing countries' in the past two decades. Moreover, they suggest that developing countries with huge debts be assisted so that their economies can catch up with richer countries and integrate more effectively at an international level.

Regardless of what IMF affirms, if the benefits of globalisation are to be more evenly spread, the goal of reducing world poverty needs to be re-prioritised. If this means imposing rules and standards on multinational companies that are acceptable internationally, then this will need to be done sooner rather than later. At this stage, the multinationals and their shareholders appear to be the only winners. The backlash against globalisation has already begun.

———————◆———————

Questions 27 – 34

Look at the following statements (Questions 27 - 34) and decide if they agree with the opinion of the writer in Reading Passage 3. Write your answers in boxes 27 - 34 on your Answer Sheet.

YES   if the statement agrees with the writer's opinion
NO   if the statement does not agree with the writer's opinion
NOT GIVEN   if the writer's opinion is not given in the text

Answer

27   Technical advances were vital in the growth and expansion of globalisation.   ....

28   World economic growth increases if countries concentrate on what they do best.   ....

29   Motivated by employment opportunities, foreign governments invited multinational companies to their shores.   ....

30   Outward-oriented government policies alone could not guarantee globalisation's success.   ....

31   Multinational companies have grown in size, but the local workers are not happy with their conditions.   ....

32   An increasing number of protests in developing nations reflects concern for the negative by-products of globalisation.   ....

33   The IMF supports globalisation and encourages all countries to globalise.   ....

34   The shareholders of multinational companies are likely to contribute towards a more even distribution of wealth.   ....

Questions 35 - 40

Using background information from the text, decide which of the statements (**A – J**) in the box below would most likely be attributed to the organisation, group, or individual in Questions 35 – 40.

Write your answers on your Answer Sheet in boxes marked 35 – 40.

STATEMENTS

A   Multinational companies can provide local and regional communities with economic support.

B   The rewards of globalisation have not been shared evenly.

C   Globalisation will spread world trade more evenly.

D   The multinational companies' success is due to the introduction and implementation of good work practices.

E   All countries participate effectively in globalisation.

F   Multinational companies are given too much autonomy.

G   Reducing world poverty should be one of the main aims of globalisation.

H   Foreign debts are limiting the participation of developing countries in globalisation.

---

35   ....   Non-government organisation

36   ....   Multinational companies

37   ....   A locally-based business

38   ....   Anti-global campaigner

39   ....   The International Monetary Fund

40   ....   The writer of the passage

PRACTICE TEST 4 - WRITING

WRITING TASK 1

You should spend about 20 minutes on this task.

> **The diagram below shows the process of distilling salty water into fresh water.**
>
> **Using the information in the diagram and the list of materials, describe the process and what is involved.**

You should write at least 150 words.

Materials:

a heat source
a pot with salty water
a metal funnel
a length of pipe
a piece of cloth

Figure 1. Process of extracting fresh water from salt water by distillation

(Source: 'The Yachtsman's Emergency Handbook: The Complete Survival Manual'
Hollander, Neil & Mertes, Harald. 1980. Angus & Robertson, US.)

WRITING TASK 2

You should spend about 40 minutes on this task.

Present a written argument to an educated reader with no specialist knowledge on the following topic:

> **Most countries offer two education systems from which parents can select the form of schooling which most suits their own child. Compare and contrast state-run and privately-owned schools in your own country or in a foreign country.**

You should use your own ideas, knowledge and experience and support your arguments with examples and relevant evidence.

You should write at least 250 words.

PRACTICE TEST 4 - SPEAKING

▶ **PART 1:**   (4 – 5 minutes) Introduction and (getting to know you) interview

Examiner: *Good morning. My name's ……….*
And your name is...? And you're from... ?
Can I see your passport please? Thank you.

- *What do you like about living in [your present country]... ?*
- *Can you tell me about your last vacation?*
- *Who do you like travelling with?*
- *Where would you like to travel to in the future?*
- *What sort of music do you like?*
- *Is music important to you?*
- *Do you like the same kind of music as your family?*

Thank you.

▶ **PART 2:**   (3 – 4 minutes) Individual long turn (monologue)

Examiner: *Now I'm going to give you a card with some information about **ADVERTISING**.*
*You will have one minute to read the card and then I'd like you to talk about **ADVERTISING***
for one or two minutes. All right? You can make some notes to help you if you wish.

Describe an advertisement that you have seen recently.

You should say:

what the advertisement was about

where you saw or heard the advertisement

how effective the advertisment was

...and explain how you felt about the advertisement.

Examiner: *Would you like to start now?*

You give your talk and after 1 or 2 minutes the examiner will ask you a question or two.

- *What's the most popular form of advertising in your country?*
- *Would you like to work for an advertising company?*

Thank you.

▶ **PART 3:**   (4 – 5 minutes) Two way discussion (more abstract conversation)

Examiner: *Now I'd like to ask you a few more questions.*

- *Is there too much advertising?*
- *Do you agree that advertisements for smoking and drinking alcohol should be banned?*
- *Certain products can only be advertised in restricted time-slots on television. Is this sort of restriction necessary?*
- *What role does advertising play in your society?*
- *How has advertising contributed to globalisation?*
- *How might advertising change in the future?*

Thank you very much.
That's the end of the speaking test. Goodbye.

ANSWER KEYS

NB: · answer words in brackets are optional
      · alternative answers are separated with a stroke (/)

PRACTICE TEST 1:

Listening

1	£203	21	A
2	17	22	B
3	no	23	A or E
4	under 26 / less than 26	24	E or A
5	locals / local people	25	C or D
6	satisfied / OK	26	D or C
7	(British) students	27	Early Childhood
8	(too) many / much / big	28	the differences / how they differ
9	careful / mindful of	29	not learned / innate
10	the culture / the food	30	in person
11	International Student Advisor	31	higher
12	learning / study groups	32	exam performance / results
13	Student IT Department	33	sleep / sleeping / sleeplessness
14	Housing Officer / Accommodation Officer	34	controlled
15	International Department	35	thought / thinking
16	personal &/or financial	36	organised
17	B	37	vary / change / be different
18	D	38	marks / weighting
19	E	39	relaxed
20	C	40	(effective) study skills

Reading

1	B	28	II
2	A	29	I
3	D	30	V
4	G	31	IV
5	H	32	mass tourism
6	E	33	the benefits / advantages
7	nuclear fusion	34	low key / smaller scale developments
8	core	35	unethical tour operators / ecotourism operators
9	starts to die	36	nature itself / nature alone / natural attractions
10	explode / collapse	37	B
11	gravity / gravitational field	38	D
12	black holes	39	C
13	debris / materials	40	D
14	(mature) green		
15	under / below / up to / less than 24		
16	within 24 hours		
17	colour / colouring (process)		
18	variation		
19	carbon dioxide / ethylene gas		
20	ethylene gas / carbon dioxide		
21	FALSE		
22	FALSE		
23	TRUE		
24	FALSE		
25	NOT GIVEN		
26	TRUE		
27	TRUE		

Answers to exercise on page 125:

1 prior   2 focus   3 speculate   4 glossary   5 logical
6 paraphrase   7 assess   8 recommend

PRACTICE TEST 1 continued:

Writing

Example answers are given for Practice Test 1 in this book. Model answers for Test 2, 3 and 4 can be found in the accompanying Study Guide to the 404 Essential Tests for IELTS.

Task 1

The table in Task 1 identifies the twelve most popular tourist attractions in the United Kingdom in 1999 and 2000.

The table clearly shows that the two newest paid-admission attractions, The Millennium Dome and The British Airways London Eye, were the most popular in 2000 with an estimated 6,516,874 and 3,300,000 visitors respectively.

In 2000, all of the other attractions with the exception of The Victoria and Albert Museum and Flamingo Land had lower numbers than in 1999. The most significant decrease was experienced at the Science Museum (-9.8%) followed closely by Madame Tussaud's (-9.5%). However, Madame Tussaud's still remains one of the top four UK paid attractions with over two million visitors in 2000. The least significant change was experienced at Chessington World of Adventures which had 1,500,000 paid visitors in 2000 and 1,550,000 in 1999.

There does not appear to be any correlation to falling numbers in city or regional areas.

(153 words)

Task 2

Discuss when, if ever, capital punishment can be viewed as a valid punishment for crime.

To many people, capital punishment is abhorrent, but it is possible to view it as a valid means of punishment. In my opinion, it can be justified as a penalty when three conditions are present. In this essay, I intend to discuss these three issues in more depth.

The rules of society are made and enforced for the purpose of protecting its members. In cases where the murder that has been committed is so frightful that society cannot allow the perpetrator back into its fold, then the death penalty may be the only answer. For example, crimes against humanity such as genocide; terrorist attacks which have resulted in many lives lost.

If the offender shows no remorse at all and is incapable of feeling any shame for his terrible actions, the only solution may be death. In these cases, it is clear that the offender cannot be rehabilitated.

Another important consideration is to ensure to the best of everyone's ability that the accused is guilty beyond reasonable doubt. If someone is punished with imprisonment, and later found to be innocent, he can be released from prison. However, when the punishment is death, it is impossible to make amends. There have been a number of examples in history where a man was found to be innocent after being hanged.

In conclusion, I believe that it is important to consider three main issues. The crime must be so bad that it would be impossible to welcome the perpetrator back into society. There must be no hope that the perpetrator can ever be rehabilitated back into society. There must be no doubt as to the perpetrator's guilt. In any situation that does not contain these components, I believe it is morally wrong to impose the death penalty.

(294 words)

PRACTICE TEST 2:

Listening

1	0278804	21	C
2	2, 5 / 5, 2 / May 2nd / 2nd May	22	B
3	17 Rocksford	23	A
4	5 p.m.	24	A
5	doorbell	25	C
6	teacher	26	G
7	pay / salary / money	27	D
8	no / break from	28	B
9	(long) summer holiday	29	A
10	by himself / by myself / alone / on his own	30	F
11	A	31	beginning and completion / ending / end
12	A	32	a schedule
13	B	33	four stages
14	B or D	34	developing a plan / planning a project
15	D or B	35	realistically
16	nearest police station	36	help / advice (from others / other people)
17	cross street / intersection	37	Gant Chart
18	café / (nearest) shop	38	standard of delivery
19	detailed / full description	39	(the) Quality Assurance
20	canceling them	40	(the / your / this week's) tutorials

Reading

1	conditions / standard(s)	28	greenhouse gases
2	(general) ill-health / disease	29	(Earth's) albedo
3	earnings / productivity / production / income	30	cumulus
4	51%	31	deforestation / land clearing
5	25%	32	F
6	weigh	33	C
7	7 million	34	B
8	anticipated	35	A
9	B	36	FALSE
10	D	37	FALSE
11	C	38	NOT GIVEN
12	A	39	TRUE
13	A	40	NOT GIVEN
14	YES		
15	NOT GIVEN		
16	YES		
17	NO		
18	YES		
19	safe		
20	side effects		
21	addictive		
22	increase		
23	small / normal		
24	difficult / hard		
25	(false) hope		
26	appropriate		
27	(possible) alternative treatment (options) / treatment options		

Writing

Example answers are given for Practice Test 1 in this book. Model answers for Test 2, 3 and 4 can be found in the accompanying Study Guide to the 404 Essential Tests for IELTS.

PRACTICE TEST 3:

Listening

1	A
2	B
3	I block
4	C block
5	student canteen / Student Canteen
6	have an interview / be interviewed
7	2 p.m. / 2 o'clock / 2:00 / 2.00
8	PASTEL
9	0412 987 35
10	BI 690011
11	C
12	C
13	A
14	9th September
15	music / opera
16	Festival Club
17	14th September
18	Performing Arts Centre
19	City Football Club
20	Under the Stars

21	C
22	329,758
23	about / over 3 million
24	75% / ¾ of population
25	friendly
26	continuing to grow / growing
27	US, Japan
28	tourism / number of tourists
29	education and technology
30	eastern and western
31	thousands of years
32	has (been) grown
33	C or E
34	E or C
35	C or E
36	E or C
37	dried fruit(s)
38	seaweed
39	cereals
40	www.vegsoc.org

Reading

1	50%
2	1988
3	monitoring (of / the) Internet / Internet monitoring
4	III
5	VII
6	VI
7	II
8	I
9	IX
10	by / via email
11	ten years
12	terrorists
13	firewalls
14	C
15	C
16	A
17	NOT GIVEN
18	NOT GIVEN
19	TRUE
20	IX
21	VIII
22	IV
23	VI
24	III
25	VII
26	I
27	V

28	degradation
29	land clearing
30	had adapted
31	water
32	water-table
33	surface
34	recharge zone
35	warning signs
36	NO
37	NOT GIVEN
38	YES
39	NO
40	YES

Writing

Example answers are given for Practice Test 1 in this book. Model answers for Test 2, 3 and 4 can be found in the accompanying Study Guide to the 404 Essential Tests for IELTS.

PRACTICE TEST 4:

Listening

1	D	21	III
2	D	22	II or VI
3	A	23	VI or II
4	A	24	IV
5	C	25	A
6	B	26	C
7	A	27	C
8	E	28	B
9	D	29	B or C

10	they are popular / of their popularity	30	C or B
11	since 1945	31	(the) state / government
12	15.25	32	noise
13	white	33	moderately windy sites / less windy sites
14	signature	34	1984
15	Internet	35	diesel generator(s)
16	$80	36	Danes / Danish
17	home country / country of issue	37	Height / height
18	a limited time / period / a year	38	1,000,000 / 1 000 000 / 1 million
19	road rules	39	twice / two times
20	fined / penalized	40	selling power (back)

Reading

1	C	28	NOT GIVEN
2	A	29	YES
3	D	30	YES
4	C	31	NOT GIVEN
5	B	32	NO
6	E	33	YES
7	A	34	NOT GIVEN
8	D	35	A
9	B	36	D
10	D	37	F
11	B	38	B
12	D	39	H
13	A	40	G

14	A
15	C
16	A
17	B
18	movement
19	characteristics
20	short term
21	slowed
22	examined
23	absent
24	genetic predisposition
25	predisposition to optimism / optimism in writing
26	high folate levels
27	YES

Writing

Example answers are given for Practice Test 1 in this book. Model answers for Test 2, 3 and 4 can be found in the accompanying Study Guide to the 404 Essential Tests for IELTS.

LISTENING TESTS TAPESCRIPTS

TEST 1

SECTION 1

You will hear two students who have just returned to university after their summer vacation. Listen to Louise and Kerry talking about their vacation.

First, look at Questions 1 – 4.

SHORT PAUSE

You will see that there is an example already done for you. For this question only the conversation relating to the example will be played first.

Kerry	Hi Louise – how was your summer vacation?
Louise	Oh fantastic – I only got back from Europe yesterday.
Kerry	Wow! That sounds exciting.
Louise	Yes, it was. How was your holiday?
Kerry	Pretty quiet compared with yours. I just stayed around Cambridge.

Louise said that she had just got back from Europe yesterday, so the correct answer is EUROPE.

Now we shall begin. You should answer the questions as you listen because you will not hear the recording a second time.

Now listen carefully and answer Questions 1 – 4.

Kerry	Hi Louise – how was your summer vacation?
Louise	Oh fantastic – I only got back from Europe yesterday.
Kerry	Wow! That sounds exciting.
Louise	Yes, it was. How was your holiday?
Kerry	Pretty quiet compared with yours. I just stayed around Cambridge – but we're planning to go to Europe at the end of next term.
Louise	Oh you'll have a great time! I really recommend it. How are you going to get around?
Kerry	Well, we've thought about renting a car. Flying is far too expensive. What did you do?
Louise	We bought Eurail tickets and traveled around Europe by train.
Kerry	Was it expensive?
Louise	No, not really. It cost us £203 for a Eurailpass Youth Ticket.
Kerry	I've heard of Eurail – what did that include?
Louise	Well, you get unlimited train travel in and between seventeen European countries. It lasted for a month.
Kerry	Gee for £203 that sounds reasonable. Did you visit all of the seventeen places?
Louise	Yes, all except for Ireland. We couldn't really understand why Ireland was included on the pass but England wasn't.
Kerry	Yes, that seems a bit strange. Did it include the trip from London to Paris in the Channel Tunnel?
Louise	No, unfortunately we had to pay extra for that train but we did get a discounted fare because we're students.
Kerry	Were there any other restrictions on the tickets?
Louise	Well, if you want to pay more or less money you can choose another plan – there are 15 and 21 day plans or 2 and 3 month plans. The only restriction for the Youth Ticket is that you have to be under 26.
Kerry	That suits my friends and me. None of us are 26 yet. We went to school together.
Louise	Oh, you really have to do it. It's safe and easy and a great way see the countryside. The weather was fantastic and so were the people!
Kerry	It sounds great.

Louise and Kerry go on to talk about traveling by train in Europe. As you listen to the rest of the conversation , answer Questions 5 – 10.

Before the conversation continues, read Questions 5 – 10.

SHORT PAUSE

Kerry	What was the best part of your trip?
Louise	The trains really gave us the freedom to plan our own holiday. We went to lots of places which were out-of-the-way and met lots of local people – you know, small rural towns where trains are still an important form of transport.
Kerry	We'd like to meet the local people – did you do that easily?
Louise	Yes, the trains in Europe aren't like the commuter trains in London. People like to talk and have a chat on trains in Europe.
Kerry	That's nice.
Louise	Yes. The train times were ok as well. Sometimes we had to get up early to catch the trains which were crossing into another country but most of the time, we were satisfied with the timetables. Very punctual.
Kerry	Should we take an alarm-clock?
Louise	Well, I would. Having an alarm clock made us sleep more comfortably. We knew that we'd wake up on time.
Kerry	And were the trains safe – did you travel at night?
Louise	Lots of students traveled at night because it saved having to pay for accommodation.
Kerry	I hadn't thought of that.
Louise	Well, lots of others have thought of it. We preferred to stay in local pubs or student hostels because you could mix with the locals. The night trains were filled with British students!
Kerry	It sounds as if you had a very positive experience. Is there anything you'd recommend we take or do?
Louise	Let me see – I can certainly tell you what not to take or do. Don't take much luggage. There just isn't very much room in the trains for big suitcases. A backpack or two small bags is better than one big bag. That way you can also get on and off the trains easily too.
Kerry	I'll remember that. My mother always says to pack one week before you go on vacation and then take half of it out the night before you leave.
Louise	That's good advice – especially when you're riding on cramped trains. The other thing is to be careful with your valuables. Lots of students had money and passports stolen – especially at night.
Kerry	Did you have anything stolen?
Louise	No but we met lots of people who did have things stolen. We all had money belts under our jackets.
Kerry	I'll have to buy one of those.
Louise	Yes, you should – or you can borrow mine if you like.
Kerry	Oh thanks – that'd be good.
Louise	The only other thing I'd advise you to do is to make sure you spend a reasonable amount of time in each country. We found that lots of students traveled too quickly and they didn't have enough time to meet the locals and enjoy the food and the culture.
Kerry	How long do you think you need in each country?
Louise	I can't say – it'll depend on who you meet and what you like to do and of course, the weather. It was so warm and sunny in some beach-side places that we stayed for four or five days. In other towns, if it was very quiet or boring, we just stayed overnight.
Kerry	I guess that's what's great about the train. You can come and go as you please.
Louise	Exactly – and it's cheaper and much more relaxing – not to mention safer – I don't think I could get used to driving on the right-hand-side of the road!

That is the end of Section 1. You now have ½ minute to check your answers.

SECTION 2

You will hear Diane Kelly, the Admissions Officer at Central City University talking to a group of newly arrived international students.

As you listen to the first part of the talk answer Questions 11 – 16.

Before you listen, look at Questions 11 – 16.

SHORT PAUSE

DIANE KELLY:

For those of you I haven't met, my name is Diane Kelly, the International Admissions Officer at Central University.

Today, I'm here to explain some of the student support services which you might like to access during your courses. The first thing I'd like to make clear is that you are all entitled to this help – all you need to do is ask for it. You have full access to all of the regular university facilities here and additional services set up exclusively for international students.

These services are grouped under four main areas of responsibility – academic support, librarian services, administrative services and those provided by the student union.

The staff in Academic Support Services is qualified to assist you in course selection, content description and explanation of assessment criteria for individual subjects. We also have an International Student Advisor who is there to help students from non-English speaking backgrounds. All of you have achieved the English requirements for entry to your particular courses but it is possible at some stage, that you will need language support. The International Student Advisor is there for that purpose. Be warned though – he is very busy at the end of semesters and he won't write your assignments for you!

If you need assistance with general study skills, the International Student Advisor will probably direct you to our library services staff. Library Services is made up of three departments – Research and Resource; Study Skills and the Student IT Department. The Study Skills Department is very active in promoting small learning and study groups. They will gladly help you to join one of these groups by matching your needs with other students.

After you get your student cards, the Student IT Department will arrange your email access and passwords for the university computers. You do need to have your student card first, so don't go there without it. Student cards are issued by Administration Officers in the Administration Student Services area.

A lot of you are in homestay at present, but if you want to move into more independent-style accommodation, see the Housing Officer at the Administration Building. Don't be too optimistic though – good, cheap accommodation close to the university is in high demand! It can be found but we advise you to see the Accommodation Officer early!

We also have a Student Employment Officer and of course the Homestay Officer, whom you would have met already.

The University Bookshop and most importantly, our International Department is in the Administration Building – so make sure that you come and see us if you have any questions about your passports or visas.

The Student Union is also very active and provides some great services. For example, if you have any personal or financial problems while you're here, the student union offers a Student Counselling Service. You will need to make appointments to see a counsellor. If you feel that you are not being treated fairly by another student or lecturer or university staff member, you might like to access the Equal Opportunity Service offered by them. They also run various social and sporting clubs and activity programs which I'd encourage you to sign up for.

Before the final part of the talk, look at Questions 17 to 20.

SHORT PAUSE

Now you will hear the rest of the talk. Answer Questions 17 to 20.

Obviously, you'll need to know where these services are. We're currently in the Grand Hall. Now if you have a look on your campus map – ah, the Library Services are of course in the library which is over to my right – just between the Outdoor Sporting Facilities and Hawkins Student Car Park. The Student Union Building is also in that same direction – but it's in front of the Car Park. For those of you who'll be travelling by bus, the university bus-stop is just outside the library.

The Administration Building is over to my left – between the International Centre and the Post Office. Most of you have been to visit us already. Even though the Administration Staff look after the Bookshop, it's in the same building as the Post Office – just behind the Student Refectory. If you come to the Administration Building, we'll show you where it is anyway.

All of the academic staff are found in their particular faculty buildings which you'll get to know very well. The Career and International Student Advisors are in a small building behind the International Centre, in between the English and the Arts Block. It's really quite easy to find your way around the campus and most staff and students are more than willing to give you directions.

Now we're just going to have a short break with some tea and biscuits at the back of the hall. So, if you'd like to stand up and come down...

That is the end of Section 2. You now have ½ minute to check your answers.

Now turn to Section 3 of your Listening Question Booklet.

SECTION 3

In this section you will hear two students discussing the Early Childhood Tutorial they are going to present.

First, look at Questions 21 to 26.

SHORT PAUSE

Now listen to the first part of the discussion and answer Questions 21 to 26.

Marie	I don't suppose you've come up with an idea for our tutorial presentation, have you?
Rose	Well, as a matter of fact, I have – I thought we could talk about the obvious differences we see between the sexes as children grow up.
Marie	Do you mean the differences we see between males and females as a result of the way they are brought up?
Rose	No, I mean the differences that exist from birth.
Marie	That sounds like a lot of work Rose ...
Rose	Not really – do you remember in our first Early Childhood lecture, we were given a list of differences which were observed in male and female babies and toddlers in the UK?
Marie	I wasn't here for the first two weeks of the semester remember? I had problems getting my passport -
Rose	Oh, that's right. Well, it was really fascinating. A group of behavioural scientists in England selected 100 children to observe over a very long period – 20 or 25 years. They were brought up in families who treated girls and boys in the same way – no special treatment for either of the sexes. They observed their play and their reactions to various situations – set up little tests I suppose.
Marie	How old were the children?
Rose	The first observations were carried out when the babies were only a few hours old – they concluded that girls were more sensitive to touch than boys at that early age!
Marie	How did they end up with that conclusion?

Rose	Well, the lecturer didn't go into detail – I think he just wanted to get our interest, you know, whet our appetite. There were lots of tests and observations done from soon after birth, right through to their early twenties. I thought we could investigate some of the case studies and then present the results in the tutorial.
Marie	That's a good idea Rose. It'll be interesting but it will also give us the chance to collect information for our end-of-term assignment as well.
Rose	It'll also be a good opportunity to check out the resources available in the library. I haven't had the chance to spend much time there yet, have you?
Marie	The last four weeks have just been so busy – and of course, I had to catch up on the two weeks that I missed – I haven't had the chance either. I've heard that the library research staff are really willing to help out.
Rose	Well, we can find out if that's true or not. We'll need to make an appointment to see them. Apparently they're in high demand.
Marie	We only have two weeks to prepare for this tutorial, so I think we should definitely start as soon as we can. Let's see the tutor this afternoon and tell him about our plan. If he agrees, we can get started on our research.
Rose	OK – I'll go and see the tutor. You can make a booking at the library.

Rose goes to the tutor's office to discuss the topic for their tutorial.

Before listening to the rest of the conversation, look at Questions 27 to 30.

Rose	Would it be possible to see Jim Clark – one of the Early Childhood tutors?
AA (Admin Assistant)	May I ask what it's about?
Rose	We have to get approval for our tutorial topics in EC101.
AA	Yes, I thought it might be about that. Unfortunately, Jim had to go to Sydney this week but he has given me some specific questions to ask about the tutorials.
Rose	Oh, we were hoping to get started on our research – we've only got two weeks.
AA	Don't worry – Jim's phoning in twice a day. If you give me the details, I can give you an answer by tomorrow morning.
Rose	That's great. We are planning to present some case studies that were undertaken by a group of…
AA	Hang on. I just need a few short details – let me see, I have to write down what the subject of the tutorial is.
Rose	OK – I guess the topic is gender and when the sexes start to act differently.
AA	So, is it about how male and female children are different? What can I write here, next to TOPIC?
Rose	Well, what about "How the sexes differ".
AA	OK – I'll put that down as your topic. Jim also wants to know the aim of your tutorial.
Rose	Well, there are two aims I suppose. The first is to show how they differ. But the other point we want to make is that the differences are innate – not learned.
AA	To – show – that – differences – between – the – sexes - are – innate – not learned. Right - that's the hard part. Now I need to know the date, time and room of your tutorial.
Rose	It's in two weeks – let's see, that'll be Tuesday 26th at 11 a.m. We are in Room B1203.
AA	And do you need any A/V material?
Rose	What does AV mean?
AA	Audio – visual – you know, TV, video, tape-recorder, overhead projector – that kind of thing.
Rose	I hadn't thought of that –guess we'll need an overhead projector. We haven't really started planning our tutorial yet – we just wanted to get initial approval from Jim.
AA	Never mind – you can always cancel the projector if you don't need it. Jim will phone in the morning – do you want to come and see me then or I can phone you if you like.
Rose	I have a lecture from 8 to 10 tomorrow morning – so I'll drop by after it finishes.
AA	Right – I'll see you then.

That is the end of Section 3. You now have ½ minute to check your answers.

Now turn to Section 4 of your Listening Question Booklet.

SECTION 4

You will hear a lecture being given by a university professor to first year students about the examination period.

First, look at Questions 31 to 40.

SHORT PAUSE

Now listen to the lecture and answer Questions 31 to 40.

Welcome to our Examinations Workshop – this is an annual event which we've found very helpful for first year students like yourselves and I hope that this year will be no exception.

By now you'll all have realized that studying at university is quite different to studying at school. Some of you might have been shocked at one time or another during the semester, when you received results for your assignments that weren't as high as you'd expected. I trust that you've spoken to your lecturers and tutors and sorted out those issues. The truth is that the transition from school to university can be a difficult one. The academic standards are higher and of course, there is considerably less supervision at university and it's incumbent on the students to follow their own study regime.

My aim today though is to help you to learn how to cope with the impending exam period by giving you some practical strategies to take with you into the exam.

We've all known students who've had a good understanding of the subject material yet failed exams or performed well-below expectations. Likewise, we've known students that have to all intents and purposes done very little work and passed with flying colours. Often these results can be put down to one thing – stress or a lack of it.

Don't underestimate the importance that stress plays in exam performance. With any exam, you should front up feeling confident, relaxed and organized. Rightly or wrongly, exams in effect, not only test your academic ability, they test your frame of mind and your ability to perform under pressure.

Stress has to be managed on two fronts – the physiological and the psychological. We all recognise that stress affects us physically – I'm sure you've all experienced an increased pulse, or sweaty hands or underarms, or shortness of breath when placed in a stressful situation. Sleeplessness can also be a problem around exam time. The most effective way to manage these physiological reactions is through controlled breathing – which we'll practise later. By controlling or regulating your breathing, you'll find that you can put yourself rather effectively into a relaxed state.

Psychologically, stress affects the way you think. For an exam you need to think rationally and this is why you need to be confident and organized before walking into the exam. Continuing to think rationally after you read an exam paper which you know nothing about is very hard to do. But if you are organized and you've put in the time needed to learn the subject material, you will have the self-control you need to think rationally. Stress can make you panic – the worst thing you can do in an exam. Look at the question calmly and rationally dissect the question. And let's face it, even if you haven't prepared well enough, you'll still need to think rationally in order to do your best under those very trying circumstances!

Just while I think of it, this is probably a good time to tell you a piece of advice that I give first year students that come to see me. Don't rely on what other students tell you about the time they allocate to study. The reports we have had over the years have been ridiculously overestimated and underestimated. Follow your own study regime and don't listen to others. We're all different, so it stands to reason that the time we need to allocate to study will be different! Generally speaking, for every hour of lectures you attend, you will need another hour of follow-up or research work if you want to achieve good grades.

Right – so where was I? We have to learn how to control our breathing and we need to have enough confidence in our ability to be able to think rationally.

Time Management is another important factor that can make or break you in an exam situation. After you have gone through the breathing exercises which you'll be familiar with, read over the entire exam noting the different marks and weighting of questions. Only after you have done this can you allocate your own time to each question. If I had a dollar for every time a student has told me that they didn't do as well in an exam as they'd hoped, because they'd run out of time I'd be rich! If you can manage your time properly in an exam, you will reduce the amount of pressure that you're under.

Anyway, note the different questions and their marks and allocate your time accordingly – as I said. Then, answer the questions that you know first. This serves to relax you further and gives you the confidence you might need to tackle the more difficult questions. However, don't spend too much time on the easy questions either – always be mindful of the time restraint and the marks that are assigned to the question.

In summary, to do well in an exam, you not only need the academic ability – you need to be in a relaxed state of mind with the ability to think clearly enough under pressure, to allocate suitable time frames to questions. If you can equip yourself with these skills and train yourself to observe time management, exam success is almost guaranteed.

We'll be holding a study skills workshop next week in the Language & Learning Centre to deal with ways in which you can study effectively for exams. You are all welcome of course.

Right, now are you ready to learn some controlled breathing exercises?

That is the end of Section 4 and the end of the Listening Test. You now have ½ minute to check your answers.

PAUSE

You now have 10 minutes to transfer your answers to your Answer Booklet.

TEST 2

SECTION 1

You will hear an external student making an appointment with a receptionist to see a counsellor at Grisham College.

First, look at Questions 1 – 5.

SHORT PAUSE

You will see that there is an example already done for you. For this question only the conversation relating to the example will be played first.

Jack	I'd like to make an appointment to see a student counsellor.
Receptionist	Yes, certainly. Are you a student at the college?
Jack	Yes – I'm studying Linguistics, 2nd year.
Receptionist	Right – I'll just get a few details.

Jack said that he is in his second year which means he is a current student – so B is the correct answer.

Now we shall begin. You should answer the questions as you listen because you will not hear the recording a second time.

Now listen carefully and answer Questions 1 – 5.

Jack	I'd like to make an appointment to see a student counsellor.
Receptionist	Yes, certainly. Are you a student at the college?
Jack	Yes – I'm studying Linguistics, 2nd year.
Receptionist	Right – I'll just get a few details. What's your student number?
Jack	0278804.
Receptionist	0 – 2 – 7 – double 8 – 0 – 4 … and there should be three letters on the end of that?
Jack	Oh yes, EXT – I guess that means external.
Receptionist	Yes, that's right. Jack Larassy – is that right?
Jack	Yes, that's me.
Receptionist	What's your date of birth Jack?
Jack	2nd May 1979.
Receptionist	Are you still living in Maldon?
Jack	No – I moved to Chelmsford last week actually.
Receptionist	What's your new address then?
Jack	17 Rocksford Avenue, Chelmsford.
Receptionist	Is that R – O – C – K – S – F – O – R – D ?
Jack	Yes, that's right The postcode for Chelmsford is CM3 94Y.
Receptionist	Thanks. What time would you like to have your interview?
Jack	When are you open?
Receptionist	The office is open from 8 a.m. to 5 p.m. but we can schedule appointments from 8 in the morning through till 7 at night.
Jack	That's great - the evening would suit me better.
Receptionist	How about 6 on Thursday night?
Jack	Terrific. Do I come here for the interview?
Receptionist	Yes, but because the office closes at 5, the door will be locked. Just ring the doorbell and the counsellor will let you in.
Jack	Where's the doorbell?
Receptionist	It's just under the sign.

Jack arrives at the Counsellor's Office for his interview and meets one of the student counsellors.

As you listen to the rest of the conversation, answer Questions 6 – 10.

Before the conversation continues, read Questions 6 – 10.

SHORT PAUSE

Counsellor	Hi – you must be Jack. I'm Ellen Short – one of the student counsellors at Grisham College.
Jack	Nice to meet you Ellen.
Counsellor	I see you're an external student Jack. Do you find it difficult to do your assignments without going to lectures?
Jack	Oh, not really. We get really good study guides that have all the information we need but we can also contact the lecturers by phone or email. It's been a great course.
Counsellor	That's good to hear. Now what can I help you with?
Jack	I'd like to talk about my career options. I'm teaching French at the moment and studying linguistics but I've been offered a research position at the university. I really don't know whether to take the position or not.
Counsellor	Oh I see. Do you enjoy teaching?
Jack	Well, yes – for the most part I do. I find teaching very satisfying – it's great to see students do well. And of course, I love the summer holiday – six weeks at the end of the school-year is fantastic.
Counsellor	Yes, but you'd get a long summer holiday at the university wouldn't you?
Jack	Yes – I think it's an even longer period.
Counsellor	Is there anything that you don't like about teaching?
Jack	Oh yes – lazy students who don't want to do any work or the ones that behave badly and disturb the rest of the class. That can be very difficult. I guess I am a little tired of teaching. The pay for teachers isn't very good either. In fact, I find it difficult to save any money from my salary.
Counsellor	I see. So, what do you think the advantages of working at the university will be?
Jack	Well, as I said, it's a research position which means I wouldn't be teaching – it would be nice to have a break. The pay will be much better than what I'm getting at the moment and of course, I'd still get a long summer holiday. And, professionally I think working at a university would help me in the future.
Counsellor	So are there any negatives?
Jack	Well, the only real negative that I can think of is that I'll be working by myself. I'm not really used to that. It seems with teaching that there's always somebody around – whether it's the students or teachers or parents.
Counsellor	So, you can only think of one disadvantage?
Jack	Well, I'd have to travel a longer distance. At the moment, I just walk to school but I'd have to drive for about 35 minutes to the university.
Counsellor	Right Jack – let's write down all of the advantages and disadvantages in both jobs.
Jack	Yes - that sounds like a good idea.
Counsellor	Right – let's start with the advantages of teaching...

That is the end of Section 1. You now have ½ minute to check your answers.

Now turn to Section 2 of your Listening Question Booklet.

SECTION 2

You will hear Constable Andrew Gray talking about a problem in the Darlinghurst area to a group of international students at The University of Technology International Centre.

As you listen to the talk answer Questions 11 – 15.

Before you listen, look at Questions 11 – 15.

SHORT PAUSE

CONSTABLE GRAY:

Before I start, I'd like to thank the University of Technology International Centre for allowing me to come and talk to you all this afternoon. The reason for my visit is to outline a problem that female international visitors and students have been having in the Darlinghurst area.

For the last month or so, thieves have been targeting the area snatching handbags and backpacks from unsuspecting women. As you probably know, Darlinghurst is very popular with tourists for shopping and sightseeing and it's also a popular meeting place for students. There are lots of cafes and coffee shops and unfortunately, we've had some thieves taking advantage of these conditions. The thieves are young and fit – they grab the bag from the woman's shoulder or out of her hand when she's involved with something else – you know, deep in conversation or window-shopping - so they grab the bag and then run away very quickly. By the time the victim realizes what's happened, the young man's out of sight and there's little hope of catching him. The victims are always female and almost always, a visitor to the area. When these incidents first started, the victims were always by themselves but now it seems they're becoming braver and targeting women in groups. Age doesn't seem to matter to the thieves – it's just a matter of opportunity. They look for someone who isn't consciously protecting their bag and for a place with an easy getaway – you know, not too crowded.

We've only had two of these bag-snatchers almost caught when the victims chased after them. Unfortunately, on both occasions, as soon as the women reached the thief, he threw the bag right at them and then escaped. One woman was hurt quite badly. They really are brazen.

We don't encourage you to chase these thieves – there are many small laneways and streets in Darlinghurst that the thieves can escape into. We just don't know what they're likely to do and we certainly don't want anyone to get hurt.

So, what can you do? Well, unfortunately, not much but we are asking that you be aware of this danger. If possible, walk with a friend while you're in the area – hang onto your bags carefully – don't leave your bags on the ground at one of the many cafes while you have a coffee or a meal and don't leave it on a chair or tabletop – in other words, be alert at all times and conscious of your bag while you're in the area.

We'd also caution you about carrying anything too valuable in your bags. Don't for instance, carry too much cash and please ensure that you know the details of all of your credit cards. It seems like the thieves are not only after cash. They've been using credit cards illegally on the Internet to purchase goods or access pornographic sites. So some of our targets not only lose the cash they have in their bags but they get a nasty surprise when their credit card bills arrive at the end of the month. It's vital that you keep your credit card details and report your loss to police.

Before the final part of the talk, look at Questions 16 to 20.

SHORT PAUSE

Now you will hear the rest of the talk. Answer Questions 16 to 20.

If you take these precautions and still get robbed, please contact your nearest police station. You can of course come to the Darlinghurst Police Station but this isn't necessary. The police will need to get certain details – in particular your name, your contact phone number and the time that the robbery took place. We'll also ask you for the exact location of the incident. Please take note of the nearest cross-street or laneway. A lot of the victims haven't been able to tell us this, but it is vital if we're going to catch these thieves - or try to remember the name of the nearest shop. We are trying to establish any patterns to the thefts. We will also need a full description of the bag or article that was snatched. Most of the bags are found discarded nearby with the cash and credit cards gone. Obviously you'll need to cancel your credit cards as a matter of urgency. The only protection you have against being made responsible for illegal use of your credit card, is if you report the card stolen before the thieves can use it.

We are confident that these thieves will stop their practice if we show that we're aware of their presence and limit their profits. The Darlinghurst police have some plain-clothes, female detectives in the area now and we're sure to catch them. Getting accurate locations of these incidents is vital.

It's not our intention to frighten any of you but we do want you to be aware of the problem and hopefully avoid any trouble.

Are there any questions?

That is the end of Section 2. You now have ½ minute to check your answers.

Now turn to Section 3 of your Listening Question Booklet.

SECTION 3

In this section you will hear two students talking to their tutor about a presentation they are going to give.

First, look at Questions 21 to 30.

SHORT PAUSE

Now listen to the discussion and answer Questions 21 to 30.

Tutor	Jane and Rick – nice to see you both. How's your presentation coming along?
Jane	Well, that's why we're here- we'd like to ask you for some clarification.
Rick	Yes, I'm afraid we are not quite sure that we understand exactly what you'd like us to include in our report.
Tutor	I'm glad that you came to see me – but the deadline is only three weeks away – are you going to have it done by then?
Jane	Oh yes – we think we've done most of the time-consuming work – we just have to pull the information from the survey together and present it in the right format.
Tutor	That's good to hear – collating is the fun part. Did you follow the steps I outlined in the questionnaire survey?
Jane	Yes. We found that the most difficult step was the first one – defining our objectives and then of course writing the items to match.
Tutor	What topic did you choose?
Rick	We decided to survey international students about their experiences and the challenges that they faced when they first came to Australia.
Tutor	Right – that's a very broad topic to survey…
Jane	We found that out the hard way.
Rick	Sure did – but we are happy with our work, aren't we Jane?
Jane	Yes, so far.
Rick	Yes, so far. We handed out almost 400 surveys to international students – not all from Longholm either. We sent 150 to Western Australian Education Department in Perth and 120 to Griffin Technical College in Melbourne.
Tutor	I'm pleased to hear that you didn't restrict the survey to Longholm.
Rick	No, we wanted to find out the responses from a range of international students in Australia, as opposed to the experiences at one tertiary institution only.
Jane	We chose a technical college as well as a university campus and a high school – that gave us access to students of different ages and different disciplines.
Tutor	So how many respondents did you get?
Jane	Well, in our trial of the survey, we received 44 out of the 50 surveys – over 88% - but that was tightly controlled. We didn't expect such a high percentage of returns from the actual survey itself. We had hoped to receive about 70%.
Rick	We were both a bit surprised really – we got over 320 surveys returned – 322 to be exact. That's 80%!
Tutor	322 out of 400 – yes that is an impressive rate of response. Did you have to do a lot of follow-up work to get those?
Rick	We sent out some postcard reminders to some students who hadn't returned the surveys by the deadline and from them we received another 38 surveys back.
Jane	Rick had written a very persuasive transmittal letter that accompanied the survey. In the letter, he appealed to their individual contributions so that the situations for international students might improve.

Tutor	Transmittal letters can be very effective – well done. So it sounds like you've followed the correct procedure up until now – you set your objectives and wrote items to match those objectives. You gave out trial surveys – collected them – chased the late surveys. I hope you had also analysed your pretest – trial results before sending out the actual surveys.
Jane	Yes, analysing the data from the trial survey was very useful. We checked all of the responses to each item in the pretest and found a pattern in some items that had been left unanswered. We re-wrote those items that were ambiguous or open to different interpretation. The actual survey worked better because of this.
Tutor	Trial surveys can be invaluable. So you sent out your transmittal letters with the survey and got a high percentage of responses. You shouldn't have any problems making conclusions for your survey.
Rick	Yes, we have collated all of our data – which took ages after we received the actual surveys back. We haven't started to make conclusions yet because we are not sure how to begin our report.
Tutor	You've done the majority of the work – as Jane said, the time-consuming part. It'll probably help you to know the three main criteria I'll be using to mark your presentations. The first is the quality of your questions' objectives – make sure that you don't give me aims of the survey. I want clear objectives for each item. The second criterion is the quality of the items in your questionnaire.
Rick	We are quite confident with the items. We analysed the pretest – trial quite thoroughly.
Tutor	Yes, you have already completed that section obviously. The third criterion will be judging the quality of your analysis of the data and the conclusions that you draw. This is always the most interesting part of the presentations for me.
Rick	Should this include percentages and tables and graphs to display the data?
Tutor	Absolutely – make your conclusions as visual as possible. They should be easy to read and easy to follow. Ensure that the tables and graphs are clearly labeled with appropriate headings and only include relevant data.
Rick	That's great – thank you very much. We know what we need to do next.
Jane	Yes – thanks a lot.
Tutor	My pleasure – I look forward to seeing your presentation in March.

That is the end of Section 3. You now have ½ minute to check your answers.

Now turn to Section 4 of your Listening Question Booklet.

SECTION 4

You will hear a lecture about Project Management being given by a university lecturer.

First, look at Questions 31 to 40.

SHORT PAUSE

Now listen to the lecture and answer Questions 31 to 40.

I'd like to begin today with a quick review of last week's lecture. We saw the definition of project management as something which has a clear beginning and a clear completion date with goals, a budget and a schedule. We saw its presence in the private and public sectors in many different industries. You'll also remember that we outlined the life cycle as it were, of a project and looked at the first of a four-stage cycle – establishing the limits of the project.

Today, we're going to talk broadly about the second stage of project management – developing a plan for the project. Next week we'll focus on the implementation of the project and then, the final stage - its evaluation.

Let's get started on today's topic though - planning the project. The success of a project will depend on the skills and care which you put in at this initial planning stage. Planning is not only necessary in terms of budget or cost, it's also crucial that you consider the time-frame of a project and the standards which you'll be expected to provide. These three elements are of course, integrated. Project-planning is best conducted as a team – you might have to take responsibility for handing over the final plan but without a team behind you, you'll find it almost impossible to plan effectively.

We'll discuss budgetary planning firstly because that is of course, what you are most likely to be evaluated on by your own manager. Before drawing up a budget, you'll need to understand the time-frame involved to carry out the work and the standard of delivery at which the labour and materials are to be supplied Now, this is arguably the most difficult to plan for. You'll never plan completely accurately for a project in terms of money but you will become better at planning realistically. And it is this part of the planning process that you will do last.

The best way to plan the cost of a project is to consider all the factors involved and how those factors relate to time and standard of delivery. Write these down on a spreadsheet format and begin the task of costing and estimating. The company that you're employed by will always have their own systems in place for doing this. They will also indicate the kind of profit they are looking for – usually in percentage terms.

The second stage of planning is the allocation of time to a project and for this, you'll have to canvass others for help. Only by asking the advice and opinions of those with expertise in the field, will you be able to establish the size of each unit of work to be completed and the order in which those units of work should be carried out. Remember that some units of work may be done simultaneously but many cannot. In your tutorials this week, you'll be introduced to the Gant Chart – that's G-A-N-T. This method of planning project activities has been very successful in the field of project management. The complete set of tasks involved in a project are identified and then planned in relation to each other. You'll soon discover that organizing and prioritizing activities is quite an art-form.

The third part of your planning as I said, will affect your money and time considerations and that is the standard of delivery that the project demands. These standards will be outlined in the tender documents if they've been your guide or the masterplan from which you're working. Always make sure that you've got ALL of the project-related documents that are available. For every unit of work that is to be completed, you'll have to write specifications – they are detailed descriptions outlining specific standards of quality in materials and labour. If these specifications are not carefully written and then complied with, the project is unlikely to be successful. These specifications will be referred to many times once the project is underway.

You will also have to deal with a Quality Assurance Manager at this stage who will advise you on the standards which need to be met. Quality management has become a valued component in successful project management companies.

I've provided you with an outline of the planning process for project management but you'll be looking at these three elements in more depth in your tutorials this week.

That is the end of Section 4 and the end of the Listening Test. You now have ½ minute to check your answers.

PAUSE

You now have 10 minutes to transfer your answers to your Answer Booklet.

TEST 3

SECTION 1

You will hear two friends talking outside an examination room about working over the vacation period. First, look at Questions 1 – 5.

SHORT PAUSE

You will see that there is an example already done for you. For this question only the conversation relating to the example will be played first.

Crystal	Hi Peter – I'm so pleased that exam's over!
Peter	Me too Crystal – I'm exhausted. I stayed up late studying last night and then got up early this morning.
Crystal	Well, you can rest now – we're on holidays for three glorious weeks.

Peter said he stayed up late studying last night, so C is the correct answer.

Now we shall begin. You should answer the questions as you listen because you will not hear the recording a second time.

Now listen carefully and answer Questions 1 – 5.

Crystal	Hi Peter – I'm so pleased that exam's over!
Peter	Me too, Crystal – I'm exhausted. I stayed up late last night studying and then got up early this morning.
Crystal	Well, you can rest now – we're on holidays for three glorious weeks.
Peter	That is a nice thought. Unfortunately though, I'm broke and if I'm going to have enough money to get through next semester, I'll have to get a job over the holidays.
Crystal	Yes, I've been thinking the same thing myself. As much as I'd like to go home to see my family, I think I'll have to get a job as well. Have you got any ideas or contacts?
Peter	Well, as a matter of fact, I'm going to go to the Student Employment Office. Do you want to come with me?
Crystal	Sure, if you don't mind. Where is it?
Peter	Let me see – (*TAKES OUT PAPER*) – I've got a map here of the campus. It's up here in Y Block.
Crystal	Oh boy – we're a long way away from there! We've just come out of N Block – here we are here.
Peter	Yes, N Block. Well, we can turn right and follow Circular Drive around but that's the long way. What's the building opposite us?
Crystal	That's the International Centre – I learnt English there before starting my Bachelor of Business.
Peter	Oh right – I see, it says I Block. I guess I stands for International. Well, let's cross Circular Drive and walk up to the right -
Crystal	No, there's lots of trees and gardens there – we'd better go to the left of the building. You can't get through otherwise.
Peter	OK – we'll head past D Block, go between B and C Blocks and then across the sports fields to Y Block.
Crystal	OK, but I'm really hungry. How about going to the student canteen before we get to Y Block? It's just on the other side of A Block – near the main entrance.
Peter	Good idea – I didn't have breakfast this morning. I'm starving! Let's go.

Peter and Crystal arrive at the Student Employment Office and the receptionist meets them.

As you listen to the rest of the conversation, answer Questions 6 – 10.

Before the conversation continues, read Questions 6 – 10.

SHORT PAUSE

Receptionist	Good morning – can I help you?
Peter	Good morning – yes, we'd both like to find some vacation work.
Receptionist	Right – for this vacation period?
Peter & Crystal	Yes. Mm – hmm.
Receptionist	Have you registered with us?
Peter & Crystal:	No.
Receptionist	Oh – you have left it a bit late. Students usually register with us around mid-semester.
Peter	Really?
Receptionist	Yes, but never mind. You will need to register, but before you do that, you'll need to be interviewed by one of our consultants.
Peter	Oh – I thought you would just give us a list of job vacancies and we would contact those places directly.
Receptionist	No, we don't give out contacts until after you've been interviewed and registered.
Peter	I see.
Receptionist	Would you like to make an appointment to have an interview?
Peter & Crystal	Yes, please. Yes – as soon as possible.
Receptionist	Let me see – today's Thursday 11th. Our consultants are here tomorrow but they are going on a Staff In-service from next Monday to Wednesday. So, it's either Friday – that's tomorrow or next Thursday.
Peter	Couldn't we see one of them this afternoon?
Receptionist	No, they are fully booked I'm afraid. End of semester is the busiest time for job placements, as you can imagine. There has been a cancellation for tomorrow morning at 9:30 or you can come after 2 tomorrow afternoon.
Peter	Can we be interviewed together?
Receptionist	Yes, I'm sure that would be ok.
Peter	Crystal, is 9:30 all right with you?
Crystal	Yes that suits me. Actually, I'm going to the dentist tomorrow – let me check the time. (*LOOKS UP DIARY*) Hang on, the dentist is at 9, so could we make it at 2?
Peter	No problem.
Receptionist	OK – that's for 2 o'clock then. What's your surname?
Peter	Pastel - P – A- S – T – E – L – Peter's my first name.
Receptionist	Thanks - and yours?
Crystal	My surname's Lu. L – U. My first name's Crystal – that's C – R – Y – S – T – A – L.
Receptionist	Right – a contact phone number please?
Peter	My mobile is 0412 987 35.
Receptionist	Thank you and I'll need your Student Number as well, so I can access your files.
Peter	Mine is B (for Business) 7 2 3 4 double 6.
Crystal	And mine is B (for Business as well) I 6 9 double zero, double 1
Receptionist	That's BI69 double 0, double 1 for you Peter and...
Crystal & Peter	No, that's mine – Wrong way around.
	(*ALL LAUGH*)
Receptionist	Oops! – it's BI69 double zero double 1 for Crystal and B7234 double 6 for Peter. I'll just put an arrow next to your names to show what I've done wrong! Right then – see you both.
Peter & Crystal	Bye. Thanks a lot.

That is the end of Section 1. You now have ½ minute to check your answers.

PAUSE

SHORT PAUSE

Now turn to Section 2 of your Listening Question Booklet.

SECTION 2

You will hear a speaker from the Brisbane Festival talking to some international visitors in Brisbane, Australia.

As you listen to the talk, answer Questions 11 – 20.

Before you listen, look at Questions 11 – 20.

SPEAKER:

Good Evening – umm, I've been asked to tell you all about the Brisbane Festival which is being held here in Brisbane from September 8th to October 6th. You are all of course, welcome to come along to the various activities that we have planned while you're visiting our city. We're happy to announce that we have some free tickets which I'll hand out later.

The Brisbane Festival is held every year in a number of venues around Brisbane, not only to show off our own local talent but also to celebrate the incredible talent that we have in the Australian and the South East Asian region. It's a great time for us to catch up with our interstate and international friends and we're thrilled that this year we have a record number of performances from South East Asian participants. We have seen an increased amount of interest from European and American artists in recent years and we welcome them as well.

Our goal is to bring people together through art by making art accessible to everyone. The Brisbane Festival aims to promote cultural understanding and interaction.

Right. Well – as you experienced today, we have a wonderful climate here in Brisbane – our average temperature is about 24°Celsius and we have something like 290 sunny days a year. Naturally we want to take advantage of this – so we've scheduled performances in public places such as Southbank Parklands and the City Gardens as well as the more traditional indoor venues – the Performing Arts Centre, Brisbane Convention Centre, the Brisbane Power House and some of our university campuses.

I'll hand out a copy of the program shortly but I'd like to tell you about some of the highlights of the program and encourage you to enjoy as many of them as possible. I can also give you details on how to get to the venues.

The first event that I'll be seeing is the Israel Philharmonic Orchestra at the Performing Arts Centre tomorrow night – that's September 8. It starts at 8 p.m. and because there is one performance only, you should get there well before 8 p.m. – say 7:30 at the latest. And then for something completely different, MONKEY which is a play - is showing at the Powerhouse at 6:30 on the following night. So you will have two late nights in a row but they are such different performances that I think you have to see both of them. MONKEY is based on a 16th Century Chinese story – you might have seen the television series... I can't wait for that one.

We also have plenty of music on the itinerary - for those of you who like to hear arias, world-renowned soprano Sumi Jo is performing with the Queensland Orchestra on September 11th. She will be starting at 8 p.m. – if you can't make it then, though, she will be performing some opera at later performances. And talking about music, Festival Club is going to be held every evening from Wednesdays to Saturdays at the City Gardens – Festival Club features music from around the world. I'm sure this will be very popular with the younger members of our group and you'll feel very relaxed in the cool, spring Brisbane evenings under the stars ... The City Gardens is one of our most popular venues.

For those of you who are interested in Visual Arts, from September 13 – no, I'm sorry September 14 – the Art Gallery will be displaying works in the Asia-Pacific Triennial. There are details of that display in the handout.

If you like drama, you'll have to see Slava's Snowshow the next day, at the Performing Arts Centre. It is a Russian production which has been wowing audiences from Moscow to London. It starts at 6 – again, don't be late because I'm sure that will be very popular and the Performing Arts Centre has limited seating.

Barbara Fordham will be performing a series of concerts at the City Football Club from September 20 – she has the most wonderful voice and you won't want to miss one of her concerts particularly if you like blues music. Concerts start at 8 – as I said at the City Football Club.

We also have a Poetry and Writers Festival happening in Brisbane if you're into that. The Poetry Festival starts on September 22th and the Writers Festival will be on from October 4 to October 6.

And if you don't go to anything else, you simply must go to the Opera Under the Stars at City Gardens. This will be the grand finale on October 6th – it really will be fantastic and I expect there will be fireworks and all sorts of exciting things going on. So remember that one, Opera Under the Stars – starting at 6 on October 6.

OK – that's it from me. I really hope that you take the time to join in whenever you can with the Brisbane Festival celebrations. If you want any more information please come and see me - the information booklets and tickets are at the front door. Have a good night everyone and enjoy your time in Brisbane.

That is the end of Section 2. You now have ½ minute to check your answers.

Now turn to Section 3 of your Listening Question Booklet.

SECTION 3

In this section you will hear two students presenting a tutorial on two Asian countries, Singapore and Malaysia.

First, look at Questions 21 to 30.

SHORT PAUSE

Now listen to the two students and answer Questions 21 to 30.

Tutor	Nancy and Jenny are presenting the first of our profiles on Asia today. You looked at Singapore and Malaysia didn't you?
Nancy	Yes, and we found lots of similarities between the two countries.
Tutor	Did you follow the outline that I gave you?
Jenny	Yes we did. Um, first of all the total land area of Singapore is 630 square kilometres, whilst Malaysia's was 329,758 square kilometres. Obviously Malaysia is a much larger nation with a bigger population – almost 24 million. It is bigger than Australia's population, in fact – we have 19,700,000. Um, Singapore, has just over 3 million.
Tutor	Did you look at their population mix?
Nancy	The population of both Malaysia and Singapore are multi-racial – they each have a mixture of Malays, Chinese, Indians and other ethnic groups as well, who all live quite harmoniously together. The breakdown of the population is different though. In Malaysia, the Malays or Bumiputeras as they are called, outnumber the Chinese and the Indians. They make up about 65% of the population. In Singapore, three quarters of the population is Chinese with only a few hundred thousand Malays and Indians. English is widely used in Malaysia as well as in Singapore.
Jenny	Yes, they all study compulsory English at school and adults use English a lot in their daily lives. For many years, Singaporeans have been sending their children abroad to study in English-speaking countries. And in recent years, Malaysians are also studying overseas and getting overseas work experience.
Tutor	Australia has had a fairly stable relationship with Singapore over the years – can you briefly talk about that?
Nancy	Umm, yes. Singapore and Australia have always maintained a friendly and warm relationship. As Jen said, many students come to Australia to study here and often they stay here to work. Similarly, lots of Australians live and work in Singapore. Singapore was one of the first Asian countries to really take advantage of its geographical location and the technological advances that were made at the end of last century. It has a strong economy.

Jenny	Singapore and Australia signed an expanded trade accord in February which covers all sorts of subjects from education through to customs procedures at the airports! It's accepted that this accord will really strengthen ties between the two countries.
Nancy	So, trade between Singapore and Australia is continuing to grow but we're not one of Singapore's top three trading partners. They're the US, Japan and Malaysia.
Jenny	Yes, and interestingly but not surprisingly I guess, Malaysia's top three trading partners are the US, Japan and Singapore.
Tutor	Yes, Singapore and Malaysia are neighbors so you would expect that. What did you discover about the relationship between Malaysia and Australia?
Jenny	Well, um, it hasn't been as stable as Singapore and Australia's friendship. Malaysians and Australians get along well on a personal level – there have been an increasing number of tourists travelling between the two countries. So, it isn't just the students who are coming here. Historically, Australia and Malaysia and for that matter Singapore as well, have a lot in common – you know, with the British Colonialists. Malaysia, now, doesn't want to blindly follow western ideas, which is fair enough.
Tutor	Yes – this is something that we'll talk about later in the semester – Australia's international relations in the region.
Jenny	There do seem to be misunderstandings and disagreements between Malaysia and Australia, but diplomats say that these are exaggerated by the media.
Tutor	Yes, we all know the power that the media has. Was there anything else?
Nancy	Well, um, yes – what I found was that Singaporeans are generally regarded as well-educated, well-travelled - knowledgeable. They enjoy a quality of life that is envied in other countries – especially in other Asian countries. The Singaporean government is spending a lot of money on education and technology.
Tutor	Is this going to continue – did you look at the government's agenda for the future?
Nancy	They are developing a knowledge-based economy. Unlike other South-East Asian countries, Singapore hasn't been dependent on the production and export of commodities. They intend to be IT driven with a highly skilled economy.
Tutor	I see and how did this differ in Malaysia?
Jenny	Well, the Malaysians are very enterprising people. They're well-educated and highly skilled too. Like the Singaporeans, they've got a strong work ethic. We both felt that of the two countries, Malaysians were much more Asian in their way of thinking, although they seem to mix Eastern and Western traditions easily. This could be one of the reasons that tourism is doing so well in Malaysia. The economy once relied almost solely on the export of raw materials, but that's changed a lot. All the experts say that Malaysia has a huge future.
Tutor	You have obviously enjoyed your research. I'm sure you'll enjoy learning more about the region as we continue on with the other overviews.

That is the end of Section 3. You now have ½ minute to check your answers.

Now turn to Section 4 of your Listening Question Booklet.

SECTION 4

You will hear an introductory lecture about vegetarianism being given by a nutritionist.

First, look at Questions 31 to 40.

SHORT PAUSE

Now listen to the lecture and answer Questions 31 to 40.

You will all have a vague understanding of what being a vegetarian is all about. Vegetarianism has been practised for thousands of years. The simplest definition is someone who doesn't eat meat of course - but does abstaining from eating meat include seafood and chicken? The fact of the matter is that people adopt the label "vegetarian" but still eat meat, at least to varying degrees. Within true vegetarianism, that is where a vegetarian is someone who doesn't eat any meat at all, there are three sub-groups. A lacto-ovo-vegetarian eats no meat but does consume dairy products and eggs. The second sub-group, lacto-vegetarians, also don't eat meat but while they will consume dairy products, they don't eat eggs. And then of course there are vegans – people with a strict vegetarian diet that don't eat any animal product or by-product including honey. In fact, they don't even wear woollen, leather or silk garments. So just keep in mind that there is an obvious sliding scale here when people talk about vegetarianism – there are those that perhaps like to think of themselves as vegetarian just because they don't eat red meat right through to those strict vegans who will only eat vegetables, fruit, beans or pulses – that is, food that have been grown.

For our purposes today, we'll be talking about vegetarians as those people who don't eat any form of meat at all – red meat, fish or poultry – but do use dairy products and eggs. Lacto-vegetarians and vegans are not the majority anyway.

With that definition in mind, let's review the myriad of reasons given for adopting a vegetarian diet. These include all sorts of preposterous theories that claim all humans should be vegetarian simply because it's natural or that humans are naturally vegetarian because biologically we resemble plant-eaters!! In the real world, vegetarians generally speaking, accept that humans are omnivores – they are capable of eating both plant and meat foods. Statistics show that the majority of vegetarians have adopted a vegetarian diet because of their religious beliefs as in the case of Hindus and Buddhists for example, or because of health-related concerns – that is, they see vegetarianism as a healthier alternative.

Look - that's not to say there aren't other reasons – some people just don't like the taste of meat and others simply can't afford to buy it. A significant number of vegetarians are animal liberationists who are against the killing of animals for human consumption. These vegetarians have taken the step of refusing to eat meat and in doing so, show that they don't condone those killings. They see the whole industry as barbaric. In the past, at least in my social circle, such a cause was seen as noble and many of us held vegetarians in high regard - they lived up to their beliefs. In more recent times, as we see the disastrous impact of introduced hooved animals on lands and the amount of resources used to feed stock at the expense of using arable land for crops, their noble cause has been ecologically justified as well. Land resources and arable lands in particular, are scarce and becoming scarcer. Perhaps it is wrong to allocate these resources to raising those animals which provide us with a food source that we can live without.

But is this the case? Can we live without meat in our diet and is living a vegetarian lifestyle indeed more healthy as advocates would have us believe? Vegetarians claim that a well-balanced vegetarian diet will supply all the essential nutrients we need to be healthy. In Western societies, as late as 20 or 30 years ago, there were many myths about vegetarianism. Those switching to vegetarianism would be warned about serious vitamin deficiencies.

Statistically though, the vegetarians are supported in their claim that vegetarians are healthier than meat-eaters. The incidence of heart disease and cancer for example, are significantly lower in non-meat-eaters. In fact it's claimed that the risks from certain cancers are reduced by up to 40% in a vegetarian diet. And let's face it, in modern Western society with our concerns regarding obesity, you don't see too many overweight vegetarians do you? Vegetarians consume less fat and protein than we do and the fat that they do consume is in the main, unsaturated – which is what has been recently labeled 'good fat'. On the other hand, animal fats tend to be saturated and an increased intake of saturated fats can lead to high cholesterol. Respiratory problems too, seem less common in vegetarians but this is also the case with meat-eaters who include a lot of fruit and vegetables in their diet. The UK Vegetarian Society's website quotes medical research has shown that on average, a lifelong vegetarian visits hospital 22% less than a meat eater.

The fact that the number of practising vegetarians has almost doubled in the last fifteen years, speaks volumes about the way our concerns for healthy living have changed. The reasons given for this increase has been according to a recent survey, 94% due to the perceived health benefits associated with a vegetarian lifestyle. Doctors and nutritionists and responsible groups like the Vegetarian Society are rightly concerned that those adopting the vegetarian diet do so in an informed way. There are health benefits to be gained by turning vegetarian, but there are also guidelines that need to be followed – Vitamin B12 for instance and recommended amounts of iron are not easily found in a vegetarian diet, and yet they are vital for healthy living.

So, where can such vitamin and mineral replacements be found in the vegetarian diet? Well, for the average vegetarian, good sources of iron are spinach, prune juice or dried fruit. Vegetarians are advised to eat these foods with fruit juices which will increase the amount of iron absorbed. B12 on the other hand, is not as readily available because it is only found to all intents and purposes in meat, fish and dairy products. This vitamin is one which vegetarians find difficult to replace. However, as I said low amounts of B12 can be found in dairy products as well as soy products or seaweed. For the stricter lacto-vegetarian and vegan, B12 can be obtained from foods that have been fortified with the vitamin. Vegetable margarines, some soy products and breakfast cereals are the most common sources.

The key to a healthy vegetarian diet is the same as any other diet – eat a wide variety of foods including grains, fruit and vegetables, beans, pulses and nuts. Vitamins and minerals must be included in the vegetarian diet, just as they have to be included in a non-vegetarian diet. You can argue all you like about vegetarians being healthier, but I'd suggest that you consider a well-balanced diet first and foremost. Whether or not you include meat is up to you. A good vegetarian diet closely matches the dietary recommendations for a healthy meat eating diet. There's an excellent website which I suggest you look at if you want further information on vegetarianism – it's www.vegsoc.org.

That is the end of Section 4 and the end of the Listening Test.

You now have ½ minute to check your answers.

PAUSE

You now have 10 minutes to transfer your answers to your Answer Booklet.

TEST 4

SECTION 1

You are going to listen to two university students talking about libraries in Australia. First, look at Questions 1 to 4.

SHORT PAUSE

You will see that there is an example already done for you. For this question only, the conversation relating to the example will be played first.

Mary Ann	What's wrong Yumi – you look very serious.
Yumi	Oh - hi Mary Ann. I've just been given the assessment guide for Law – my major – and there are lots of assignments.
Mary Ann	You'll be spending a lot of time in the library then.
Yumi	That's my problem – I don't know anything about libraries in Australia.
Mary Ann	Well, don't worry about that Yumi. Librarians here are really friendly and most of them are extremely helpful.

Yumi said she doesn't know anything about libraries in Australia. So B is the correct answer.

Now we shall begin. You should answer the questions as you listen because you will not hear the recording a second time.

Now listen carefully and answer Questions 1 – 4.

Mary Ann	What's wrong Yumi – you look very serious.
Yumi	Oh - hi Mary Ann. I've just been given the assessment guide for Law – my major – and there are lots of assignments.
Mary Ann	You'll be spending a lot of time in the library then.
Yumi	That's my problem – I don't know anything about libraries in Australia.
Mary Ann	Well, don't worry about that Yumi. Librarians here are really friendly and most of them are extremely helpful.
Yumi	That's good to hear. My flatmate said I should join the local library – do you think that I need to?
Mary Ann	Well, I think it'd be a good idea. They probably won't have many Law books in the library but you'll be surprised at what they do have. Australian libraries are generally very well-resourced and hey, if nothing else, you can get free Internet access.
Yumi	Is it easy for international students to join?
Mary Ann	Yes, Li Yun has just joined. All you need is your Student Card (or some other I.D.) and an account or bill that has your Australian address on it.
Yumi	Like a phone bill or an electricity bill – would that be ok?
Mary Ann	Yeah, that's all. It's very easy. They encourage people to join the library and you can borrow lots of books as well as video and audio tapes or CDs. The newspaper is available too if you've got time to stay at the library and read it!
Yumi	Will it cost much to join the library?
Mary Ann	Joining libraries here doesn't cost anything but you'll have to pay a fine if you return your books after the due date – it's about 10 cents per book per day.
Yumi	How long can I borrow books for?
Mary Ann	The loan period for books is about a month but you can easily extend the time for another month if you want to – you can even do it over the phone but it has to be arranged before the due date.
Yumi	What about the university library?
Mary Ann	Haven't you been there yet?
Yumi	No, not yet. I was sick for the orientation week and I missed out on the campus tour.
Mary Ann	Well, Yumi - I've got an hour before my next lecture. Why don't we walk up together and have a look around?
Yumi	Oh, that'd be great Mary Ann – I'd really appreciate it.

Yumi and Mary Ann arrive at the main entrance to the university library.

As you listen to the rest of the conversation, answer Questions 5 – 10.

Before the conversation continues, read Questions 5 to 10.

SHORT PAUSE

Mary Ann	This is the main entrance. Let's go in.
Yumi	It's very big isn't it?
Mary Ann	Yes, but here's a map which will help you. Can you see that it's a kind of L shape?
Yumi	Oh yes. Is that the Circulations Desk in front of us?
Mary Ann	Yes, that's where all of the incoming and outgoing loans are registered. When you return a book, just put it in the large box over there – see it's marked RETURNS – just to the right of the desk.
Yumi	Yes I see. Can I use the computers behind the desk to access the Internet?
Mary Ann	Those computers are for the library's data-base search system only. There are computers in the IT Block which we passed on our way here to the library. Anyway, you can search for a book by typing in the title, author, topic or a key word.
Yumi	Are the computers easy to use?
Mary Ann	Yes, very easy. Even I can use them!
Yumi	Does it give a catalogue number after you do the search?
Mary Ann	Yes it does. It'll also tell you in which section of the library to find the book. The library is divided into three sections – straight ahead, behind the Circulations Desk is the Monograph Collection – that just means you can borrow these materials for normal loans.
Yumi	Monograph Collection? Yes, I see.
Mary Ann	The section behind the photocopiers is for all of the Serial Publications – that means journals and magazines and newspapers of course.
Yumi	Mm hmm.
Mary Ann	And the most important section for us is the Reference Section – you'll use it a lot! Unfortunately, the books in this section can't be borrowed – you have to use them in the library. It's over there, past the quiet study area.
Yumi	I see. So do I need to join or register here, or do I have automatic borrowing rights as a student?
Mary Ann	As long as you have your student card, you can borrow books from the Monograph Collection. Anyone else can access the rest of the library.
Yumi	What if I can't find a particular book?
Mary Ann	That's what the staff are there for Yumi. Just go to the Advisors' Desk, take a request card and fill in the details of what you are looking for.
Yumi	Where's the Advisors' Desk?
Mary Ann	It's just over there – the desk at the entrance to the Quiet Study Area.
Yumi	Right – well, I think I'll have a look now to see if I can find any of the Recommended Texts for my first Law Assignment.
Mary Ann	Yes, good idea. Texts on the recommended lists from lecturers are very popular and you should try to borrow them from the library as soon as you get your list.

That is the end of Section 1. You now have ½ minute to check your answers.

Now turn to Section 2 of your Listening Question Booklet.

SECTION 2

You will hear Inspector Jack Dunne talking about International Drivers' Licenses at an information session for international travelers.

As you listen to the first part of the talk answer Questions 11 – 16.

Before you listen, look at Questions 11 – 16.

SHORT PAUSE

JACK DUNNE:

I'm sure that you have all heard about International Driving Licenses. They've been around since 1949, when the United Nations gave approval for their use. This meant that travelers could drive freely in the 186 countries that recognise the International Driving License system – regardless of the language that the drivers spoke. The only conditions were that the driver had to already hold a driving license in their home country and they had to be at least 18 years of age.

International Driver's Licenses are well-recognised – after all, they've been in use for over 50 years! To break the language barrier, the license is printed in 11 different languages but the last page of the booklet is always in French. As I said, it is a booklet – about the size of a passport – um, 10.8 by 15.25 centimetres to be exact. So it is easy to carry with your travel documents. It's not too thick or heavy either. Only seventeen pages. All of the pages are coloured white but the cover of the license is gray. It is a useful form of identification when you travel because it includes a passport-sized photograph and the driver's signature.

The International Driver's License can only be purchased from authorized travel associations in different countries but it can also be ordered on the Internet.

The cost of course varies from country to country and for the term or the duration of the license – for example, a one year license might cost approximately $40 whereas a three year license costs double that. A five year license will set you back about $100.

Before the final part of the talk, look at Questions 17 to 20.

SHORT PAUSE

Now you will hear the rest of the talk. Answer Questions 17 to 20.

Before I outline the four most important points to consider before rushing off to get your International Driver's License I should probably mention that yes, the International Driver's License covers all types of vehicles from motorbikes to trucks – but just as in your own country, you have to be qualified to drive such vehicles. You might like the idea of driving around the Australian outback on a motorbike or checking out the English countryside in a bus with all your mates, but you'll have to take the appropriate test before you set off!

OK – now the four main points - firstly, you cannot use an International License in the country in which it is issued – it is for international travel only. Some international students avoid this rule by ordering their licenses on the Internet which will ask them to nominate a 'country of your choice' for that very purpose.

Secondly, some countries won't allow you to use an International License indefinitely. In Australia for example, you can only use the International License for a year – after that you must get an Australian Driving License. Other countries aren't as strict as that

Drivers on International Licenses must abide by the road-rules in the country that they are visiting. If you are caught breaking those road rules, you will have to pay the penalty – usually a fine. And if you are the cause of an accident, expect to pay for any damages that you are responsible for. Holding an International Driver's License does not give you the right to be reckless.

And yes, if you have been suspended or banned from driving in your own country, the same rules apply with an International Driver's License – you must have an existing Driver's License to apply for an International Driver's License. Some police will in fact, want to see both your International License and your own Driver's License – so carry both licenses with you to save wasting valuable time.

Finally, you don't have to take another driving test to get an International Driver's License – your own Driver's License is proof that you know how to drive. However, it is your responsibility to learn the road-rules of the country that you are visiting and to understand what the different road-signs mean. Police are not always understanding to foreign drivers! If you break road-rules either deliberately or out of ignorance, expect to pay the price. Police are ultimately the same everywhere.

That is the end of Section 2. You now have ½ minute to check your answers.

Now turn to Section 3 of your Listening Question Booklet.

SECTION 3

In this section you will hear two students discussing the idea of joining a learning circle.

First, look at Questions 21 to 30.

SHORT PAUSE

Now listen to the discussion and answer Questions 21 to 30.

Anita	What's the reason for the learning circle you've set up Hamish?
Hamish	Well, it wasn't my idea - the Economics tutor suggested it actually – he said that it's a good way to make sure you put in the time needed for a particular subject. But for me, well, I thought that studying in a group like that would give me some incentive to study – I really need a reason to learn, you know, motivation, especially in economics!
Anita	Hmm, I guess study groups can give you discipline and motivation. They're both useful but my biggest problem is that I'm finding economics quite difficult. I think I need extra help just to understand the material. A learning circle could help - I was thinking of even getting a private tutor.
Hamish	Private tutors can be expensive – you're welcome to join us and it won't cost you anything. Every week we're going to begin the session with problems and questions from material that we've been given in the lecture. We want the learning circle to be practical and worthwhile, so that we all help each other to do well.
Anita	Do you think the others in the group would mind if I joined as well?
Hamish	Of course not – there are only five of us and you know us all.
Anita	I've been researching some past exam papers, so I'd be happy to contribute those to the circle if I join.
Hamish	One of the others suggested doing that too. He thought that we should try and identify any trends or common questions that were included in the past papers and that way we could prepare a little better for the final exam.
Anita	Yeah, that's what I was thinking. In fact, I've already started looking at last year's exams.
Hamish	Great – we're also going to hold mock tutorials, so we can practise our presentations on a smaller group before we have to do the real thing.
Anita	I am so worried about that. I'm dreading that first presentation – I've never done any kind of public speaking before.
Hamish	Well, you're not alone – I think we're all pretty nervous about it but we're hoping that the mocks will give us all a bit of confidence for the real tutorial. We don't want the group to be competitive – just collaborative – you know, working together and helping each other.
Anita	It sounds like you've really thought the learning circle idea through – you seem well-planned.
Hamish	It's just that when we all met last week to discuss the idea, we all had a list of objectives – you know, what we wanted to get out of a learning circle. That made the planning quite easy. Look, why don't you come next week to our first circle and you

can see if it's what you're looking for. If not, well, you won't have lost anything and you can always organize a tutor for yourself afterwards.

Anita Yeah, I think I will. When and where are you going to meet?

Hamish Our inaugural meeting of the circle is on Thursday evening – from 6 to 8 in Ryan Hall.

Anita OK – I'll be there.

Hamish We plan to talk about any material that we've had trouble with from the lecture first and then, we thought we'd talk about our individual learning styles. Even though we all know each other as friends, we thought that because it'll be our first time together as a study group, it might be useful.

Anita I'm not exactly sure what my learning style is!

Hamish Give it some thought during the week and try to notice how you study – some people summarise everything or re-write lecture notes every week – others like to highlight the important points or group similar bits of information together. People like me – well, I have to read material at least three times before I can really comprehend it.

Anita Really? I'm a writer I guess – I have to write everything down or I forget it straight away! I use the computer a lot.

Hamish See – you do know how you learn – you just had to think about it.

Anita I'll bring the exam papers and the research that I've started.

Hamish We probably won't have time to look through them at our first meeting.

Anita I'll bring them anyway – just in case. I think this learning circle idea is going to be a great success!

That is the end of Section 3. You now have ½ minute to check your answers.

Now turn to Section 4 of your Listening Question Booklet.

SECTION 4

You will hear a guest speaker at an Alternative Energy Seminar talking about wind-power.

First, look at Questions 31 to 40.

SHORT PAUSE

Now listen to the talk and answer Questions 31 to 40.

Good morning – thank you for giving me the opportunity to speak at this year's alternative energy seminar.

Right. Well – I know that the next speaker, John Dunkett, is going to talk about the mechanics of generating power using wind as an alternative source of energy, so I won't be using any technical terms and I won't be going into the technology of how wind generators actually work. I'll be concentrating on sharing my own experiences with you. For those of you who don't know, I live on a very windy farm some 3000 kilometres from the nearest city. That means we are not connected to the State Electricity Commission's grid and we have to produce our own electricity. When I first bought the farm in 1975, we got our electricity supply exclusively from diesel and petrol generators. The problems with this were two-fold: a lot of fuel was wasted because the generators usually didn't run to their full capacity and more importantly to my wife, the generators were extremely noisy – especially at night.

After we'd been on the farm for about six months, I heard about what they called a Hybrid System. This meant that we could keep the diesel generator but we also got a generator that was powered by wind. Because our place is so consistently windy – especially in summer – our hybrid system worked very well. In fact, we couldn't believe how well it worked!

We also had friends closer to the city who bought this hybrid system at the same time, and they were very pleased with the efficiency of it as well. Their farm is considerably less windy than ours – so even in moderately windy sites, the hybrid system appeared to work well.

Both of us agreed that we made substantial savings in fuel at the end of the first year and of course, our wives were happier – because it wasn't as noisy, as often!

In 1984, we found that we were rarely using our diesel generator and decided to try our hand at becoming self-sufficient in wind-generated power. We were sure that we'd survive without the back-up of the diesel generator, so we imported four wind generators from Denmark. America and Australia were dabbling in the technology, but we were too far behind the Europeans. The benefits of wind generators were much more obvious to the Danes and now as a result, they supply about 50% of wind turbines around the world.

Anyway, the Danish wind generators had a rated power output of 55 kilowatts per generator. They made quite an impact on our landscape and even though we could sometimes hear the mechanical noise from the generator itself, they were very quiet. The rotor diameters were about 20 metres. We felt proud that we were only using energy from clear, moving air to generate our electricity – no diesel or petrol or fuel smells either! We knew that our resource was renewable – we are after all, not going to run out of wind, especially at our place. The wind turbine is used to charge-up batteries which store the energy.

Last year, we bought a 600-kilowatt machine – it is about 46 metres high with a rotor-diameter of 43.5 metres. We found that the cost of the turbine was recovered within about 8 months. It should produce over 1,000,000 kilowatt hours per year for us. We expect it to last for about twenty years with regular six-monthly maintenance. It does look a bit strange against our flat terrain but we love it. Best of all, my wife says she can't even hear the "windmill" as she calls it, from our house at night. Frankly, I think her hearing just isn't what it used to be – but I must agree that it is very quiet. Additionally, we expect it to last for about 20 years with regular maintenance.

Our farm is isolated and yet, you'd be amazed by the number of visitors we have each year to inspect our wind turbines and the effectiveness of the wind generators. Actually, we often joke that when we stop making money from the farm, we'll charge tourists to come and visit our very own wind-farm. There is also the possibility of selling the electricity that we generate back to the electricity commission but I think that is all in the future. We've had a lot of people ask us why we chose wind-power generated energy rather than solar energy but as soon as they visit our windy farm, they know why. Even if our farm were not as windy as it is, we'd make that choice again. From all accounts, it is the least expensive form of renewable energy technology that we have. It can be used in a variety of applications from isolated farms such as ours, to supplying small sailboats without power.

Now, I'll hand you over to John Dunkett from the Danish company that sold us our original four wind turbines and he'll explain how this remarkable technology has developed over the last 20 or 30 years.

That is the end of Section 4 and the end of the Listening Test. You now have ½ minute to check your answers.

PAUSE

You now have 10 minutes to transfer your answers to your Answer Booklet.

SCORE ANALYSER - READING & LISTENING

After completing each of the *404 Essential Tests for IELTS* practice tests, use the Score Analyser to see

    a.   if your results are higher in the earlier sections than the later sections of the tests, or

    b.   if your errors are made in certain question types.

Follow the three steps outlined below to analyse your errors.

Step 1   Firstly, record your result for each section in the reading and listening tests.

TEST 1

TEST 1	Listening		
Section	Questions	Total	Your Score
1	1 - 10		
2	11 - 20		
3	21 - 30		
4	31 - 40		
		40	

TEST 1	Reading		
Passage	Questions	Total	Your Score
1	1 - 13	13	
2	14 - 27	14	
3	28 - 40	13	
		40	

TEST 2

TEST 2	Listening		
Section	Questions	Total	Your Score
1	1 - 10		
2	11 - 20		
3	21 - 30		
4	31 - 40		
		40	

TEST 2	Reading		
Passage	Questions	Total	Your Score
1	1 - 13	13	
2	14 - 27	14	
3	28 - 40	13	
		40	

TEST 3

TEST 3	Listening		
Section	Questions	Total	Your Score
1	1 - 10		
2	11 - 20		
3	21 - 30		
4	31 - 40		
		40	

TEST 3	Reading		
Passage	Questions	Total	Your Score
1	1 - 13	13	
2	14 - 27	14	
3	28 - 40	13	
		40	

TEST 4

TEST 4	Listening		
Section	Questions	Total	Your Score
1	1 - 10		
2	11 - 20		
3	21 - 30		
4	31 - 40		
		40	

TEST 4	Reading		
Passage	Questions	Total	Your Score
1	1 - 13	13	
2	14 - 27	14	
3	28 - 40	13	
		40	

☞ Your results should be higher in the earlier sections of the tests than the later sections of the tests.

SCORE ANALYSER - READING & LISTENING continued

Step 2

Secondly, write the number of incorrect answers you made in each of the question sets below.

Then, note the question type in which your incorrect answers occur.

Use this to study whether or not there is a pattern to your mistakes and give yourself opportunities to practise the question types that you find difficult.

TEST 1

TEST 1	Listening		
Question Types	Question Sets	Total	Total incorrect
Completing sentences	5 - 10 31 - 32 37 - 40	12	
Completing tables	11 - 16 27 - 30 33 - 36	14	
Labelling	17 - 20	4	
Multiple choice	21 - 22	2	
Multiple choice x 2	23 - 26	4	
Short-answer	1 - 4	4	
		40	

TEST 1	Reading		
Question Types	Question Sets	Total	Total incorrect
Completing a flow chart	17 - 20	4	
Completing sentences	7 - 13 14 - 16 32 - 36	15	
Heading bank	28 - 31	4	
Matching	1 - 6	6	
Multiple choice	37 - 40	4	
Identifying viewpoints, facts and opinions	21 - 27	7	
		40	

TEST 2

TEST 2	Listening		
Question Types	Question Sets	Total	Total incorrect
Completing sentences	16 - 20 26 - 30	10	
Completing summaries	31 - 34	4	
Completing tables	1 - 5 6 - 10 35 - 39	15	
Multiple choice	11 - 13 21 - 25	8	
Multiple choice x 2	14 - 15	2	
Short-answer	40	1	
		40	

TEST 2	Reading		
Question Types	Question Sets	Total	Total incorrect
Completing sentences	1 - 8 28 - 31	12	
Completing summaries	19 - 27	9	
Matching	32 - 35	4	
Multiple choice	9 - 13	5	
Identifying viewpoints, facts and opinions	14 - 18 36 - 40	10	
		40	

Step 2 continued

TEST 3

TEST 3	Listening		
Question Types	Question Sets	Total	Total incorrect
Completing sentences	6 - 7 25 - 30 31 - 32 40	11	
Completing tables	8 - 10 14 - 20 22 - 24 37 - 39	16	
Labelling	3 - 5	3	
Multiple choice	1 - 2 11 - 13 21	6	
Multiple choice x 2	33 - 36	4	
		40	

TEST 3	Reading		
Question Types	Question Sets	Total	Total incorrect
Completing sentences	1 - 3 10 - 13	7	
Completing summaries	28 - 35	8	
Heading bank	4 - 9	6	
Matching	20 - 27	8	
Multiple choice	14 - 16	3	
Identifying viewpoints, facts and opinions	17 - 19 36 - 40	8	
		40	

TEST 4

TEST 4	Listening		
Question Types	Question Sets	Total	Total incorrect
Completing sentences	10 31 - 32 40	4	
Completing summaries	17 - 20	4	
Completing tables	11 - 16 33 - 36 37 - 39	13	
Labelling	5 - 9	5	
Matching	21 - 24	4	
Multiple choice	1 - 4 25 - 27 28	8	
Multiple choice x 2	29 - 30	2	
		40	

TEST 4	Reading		
Question Types	Question Sets	Total	Total incorrect
Completing sentences	18 - 24	7	
Completing summaries	25 - 26	2	
Matching	1 - 8 14 - 17 35 - 40	18	
Multiple choice	9 - 13	5	
Identifying viewpoints, facts and opinions	27 - 34	8	
		40	

SCORE ANALYSER - READING & LISTENING continued

Step 3   **Thirdly, check your scores on the Score Interpreter below.** This will give you a good idea of the level of English you are currently at, and whether you will need additional English study before taking the IELTS test or applying for entry to a tertiary institution.

When looking at your results, don't worry too much if you don't improve with every practice test. There may be some tests, and some sections in tests, that you will find easier than others due to your English vocabulary or your understanding of the subject.

Remember that this Score Interpreter should be used as a guide for your reading and listening ability only. It was compiled after thorough analysis of the trial results undertaken with the *404 Essential Practice Tests for IELTS.* It provides a good indication of your ability and potential to do well but remember that a good score here is no guarantee of a good score in the actual IELTS test.

Score Interpreter

No. of correct answers	Implications
0 - 7	You will need at least 30 weeks of intensive, formal, full-time English study before attempting the IELTS test. A score like this indicates that you need to improve your knowledge of English vocabulary, your reading speed in English and your listening. Moreover, it is very likely that your other skills will also need much improvement. Don't attempt any more practice tests until you have done some more English study. Read the advice in *101 Helpful Hints for IELTS*.
8 - 15	You will need at least 20 weeks of intensive, formal, full-time English study before attempting the IELTS test. There is much you can do to help improve your English. Use the Score Analyser to discover if your difficulties result from a specific or systematic problem, or the time restrictions. By targeting your problem areas, you can focus on improvement. Try some other reading practice before taking the next practice test. Complete the exercises in *202 Useful Exercises for IELTS*.
16 - 23	You will need to study for at least another 10 weeks of intensive English before taking the IELTS test. Increase your exposure to other reading texts and listen more to English being spoken. Do not just complete the practice tests. Also see the suggestions made in the Introduction to *404 Essential Tests for IELTS* – in particular, try the Immersion Ideas that are outlined.
24 - 28	This score indicates a good level of English. It should be sufficient to gain acceptance into an Academic English preparation program for university entrance, or directly into a foundation or diploma course. With a little more study and practice <u>before</u> you take the IELTS test, you could improve enough to get directly into your chosen course.
29 - 34	This is a very good score and it should be good enough for you to gain acceptance into the course of your choice, dependent upon the requirements of the institution you are applying to. If you are getting these scores in this area for all of the tests in this book, then you are more than ready to attempt the IELTS test.
35 - 40	Well done! This score shows that you have an excellent knowledge of English. If your score in reading and listening can be matched in the speaking and writing sections of the IELTS test, you would be more than able to cope with studying in an English speaking institution. Pack your bags!

 Always check with the particular institution that you are dealing with as entry requirements differ according to the course, the faculty, the institution and the country you plan to study in.

IELTS LISTENING TEST 1 2 3 4 **ANSWER SHEET**

Question
Number: Answer: Name: ....

Question Number	Answer				Question Number	Answer		
1		▭	1	▭	22		▭	22	▭
2		▭	2	▭	23		▭	23	▭
3		▭	3	▭	24		▭	24	▭
4		▭	4	▭	25		▭	25	▭
5		▭	5	▭	26		▭	26	▭
6		▭	6	▭	27		▭	27	▭
7		▭	7	▭	28		▭	28	▭
8		▭	8	▭	29		▭	29	▭
9		▭	9	▭	30		▭	30	▭
10		▭	10	▭	31		▭	31	▭
11		▭	11	▭	32		▭	32	▭
12		▭	12	▭	33		▭	33	▭
13		▭	13	▭	34		▭	34	▭
14		▭	14	▭	35		▭	35	▭
15		▭	15	▭	36		▭	36	▭
16		▭	16	▭	37		▭	37	▭
17		▭	17	▭	38		▭	38	▭
18		▭	18	▭	39		▭	39	▭
19		▭	19	▭	40		▭	40	▭
20		▭	20	▭					
21		▭	21	▭					

Listening Total:	
Band Score	
Marker's Initials	

~ For use with the 404 Essential Tests for IELTS ~

IELTS READING TEST **ANSWER SHEET**

Question
Number: Answer: Name: ....

1		▭ 1 ▭		22		▭ 22 ▭
2		▭ 2 ▭		23		▭ 23 ▭
3		▭ 3 ▭		24		▭ 24 ▭
4		▭ 4 ▭		25		▭ 25 ▭
5		▭ 5 ▭		26		▭ 26 ▭
6		▭ 6 ▭		27		▭ 27 ▭
7		▭ 7 ▭		28		▭ 28 ▭
8		▭ 8 ▭		29		▭ 29 ▭
9		▭ 9 ▭		30		▭ 30 ▭
10		▭ 10 ▭		31		▭ 31 ▭
11		▭ 11 ▭		32		▭ 32 ▭
12		▭ 12 ▭		33		▭ 33 ▭
13		▭ 13 ▭		34		▭ 34 ▭
14		▭ 14 ▭		35		▭ 35 ▭
15		▭ 15 ▭		36		▭ 36 ▭
16		▭ 16 ▭		37		▭ 37 ▭
17		▭ 17 ▭		38		▭ 38 ▭
18		▭ 18 ▭		39		▭ 39 ▭
19		▭ 19 ▭		40		▭ 40 ▭
20		▭ 20 ▭				
21		▭ 21 ▭				

Reading Total:	
Band Score	
Marker's Initials	

~ For use with the 404 Essential Tests for IELTS ~

IELTS WRITING TEST ANSWER SHEET

Name: ....

....

....

....

....

....

....

....

....

....

....

....

....

....

....

....

....

....

....

....

....

~ For use with the 404 Essential Tests for IELTS ~

~ *For use with the 404 Essential Tests for IELTS* ~

GLOSSARY OF TERMS

Check the meaning and spelling of the following words and phrases in a good English dictionary...

(The terms are not specific to one test. To avoid repetition they are listed where they first occur.)

...IN ESSENTIAL PRACTICE TEST 1

abide	inevitable
allocation	installed
anticipate	invented
apparent	irrational
aspects	longevity
assumption	magnet
atoms	mass
belongings	minute *(adj)*
capacity	misconception
circulation	moisture
collapse	petition
component	phase
concept	physiological
condone	potential
conservation	psychological
conservatively	random
core	regulate
dense	resource
discovered	stabilize
ecosystem	strict
engulf	subsequent
environmentalist	survive
eventually	sustainable
evidence	target
expand	thermostat
exploitation	trend
fauna	unforeseen
flora	valid
gravity	valve
habitat	ventilation
harassment	....
hazard	....
host	....
impact	....
incidence	....
incorporate	....
indigenous	....

...IN ESSENTIAL PRACTICE TEST 2

accessible	overstate
addiction	percentage
addictive	pharmaceutical
ailment	phenomena
atmosphere	prescription
attributed	prestigious
boil down to	prevalent
causal	preventable
cautious	productivity
compile	pursue
comprehensive	questionnaire
counselling	radiation
data	reform
debate	regional
distribution	respect
donor	resultant
dose	sociologist
emotive	stagger
eradicate	strategy
expert	survey
external	tender *(n)*
fatal	vapour
fossil fuels	visible
frustrated	....
fundamental	....
global	....
illegal	....
imbalance	....
incentive	....
incident	....
insufficient	....
interaction	....
marketed	....
mortality	....
objectives	....
outline	....
overall	....

GLOSSARY OF TERMS continued

...IN ESSENTIAL PRACTICE TEST 3

accumulate
adapt
adversely
annual
aquatic
bear in mind
biological
canvass
conduct
consequence
contract
counteract
crop
cultivated
cyber
deficiency
degradation
detect
detrimental
diagnose
disease
disorder
diversity
essential
evaporate
extensive
fibrous
firewall
generate
hacker
hormones
implement
intruder
legislation
leisure
life-threatening
malicious
monitor
near miss

precautionary
previous
probation
profile
recovery
relatively
remediate
salinity
schedule
sector
short-sighted
sponsor
technology
time-consuming
tobacco
tolerant
tolerate
unaware
useless
vegetation
version
....
....
....
....
....
....
....
....
....
....
....
....
....
....
....
....
....
....

...IN ESSENTIAL PRACTICE TEST 4

accuse
authorized
campaign
carry out
cognitive
commute
complex
contentious
correlation
debt
decade
decline
deter
diameter
digest
domestic
equitable
evaluate
excessive
expectancy
flatmate
globalisation
gulf
imminent
inextricable
intellectual
invaluable
librarian
loan
lobby
motivate
multinationals
multitude
negligible
ongoing
onset
orientation
persuade
poverty

predisposition
progressive
proposition
protest
pull out
reflect
regret
respond
restrict
retain
scourge
severity
symbol
tutor
....
....
....
....
....
....
....
....
....
....
....
....
....
....
....
....
....
....
....
....

GLOSSARY OF TERMS continued

according to	compensate	discuss	focus	monologue	report
alternative	consequences	distinct	glossary	narrate	requirements
analyse	consider	eliminate	headings	ongoing	sequence
appropriate	contradict	evaluate	highlight	paraphrase	speculate
assess	contrast	exemplify	identify	penalize	statistics
assignment	correlation	exhibit	illustrate	precede	systematic
candidate	correspond	expertise	immerse	precise	summary
classify	degree	explain	justify	prior	synonym
cloze	describe	extent	label	procedure	theme
colleague	diagram	factor	logical	prompt	tutorial
compare	dialogue	flow chart	mention	recommend	valid

Table of words often used in instructions in the IELTS examinations and in explanatory guides such as the Introduction section of this book and the *Study Guides to the 404 Essential Tests for IELTS*.

Sentence Completion Exercise:

Complete the sentences below using the words in the table above. The answers are given on page 84.

1. After taking these practice tests and .... to taking the actual IELTS test, analyse your answers carefully and set yourself a realistic study plan.

2. Don't be distracted by other candidates in the test. It is imperative to .... on the task at hand and keep your concentration.

3. Learning to predict and to .... about what might be discussed by reading the instructions or given information in a test are valuable listening techniques.

4. If there are technical or unfamiliar words in a reading passage, look at the .... for meanings that might help your understanding of the content.

5. Before the end of a test, make .... guesses to any questions that you cannot answer. Rely on your own common sense and background knowledge.

6. Being able to .... or use different words to express the same idea is necessary in any academic writing.

7. Speaking examiners can only .... your ability during the interview. He/she must rely completely on your performance in that interview.

8. We strongly .... that you follow the General Pointers and Immersion Ideas outlined in *404 Essential Tests for IELTS* in order to improve your chances in the IELTS test.

AND AUSTEN PRESS

ADAMS

STUDY GUIDES

to the

404

Essential Tests for

IELTS

INTERNATIONAL EDITION

FOR STUDENTS WHO ARE SERIOUS ABOUT OBTAINING A HIGH IELTS SCORE

BY DONNA SCOVELL, VICKIE PASTELLAS, & MAX KNOBEL

Audio CD

Cassette

Book

Academic Module Study Guide

"Study Guide to the 404 Essential Tests for IELTS" is a detailed guide to IELTS based on the 404 Essential Practice Tests. With Model Answers for the Speaking Tests and all of the writing tasks in 404, it focuses on developing the necessary skills to maximise performance in the IELTS test. Structured activities and extra questions are provided to give serious candidates more opportunities for practice. Detailed descriptions for the reading and listening tests are also included. Four speaking interviews are provided on the accompanying cassette / CD.

General Training Module Study Guide

Audio CD

Cassette

Book

Study Guide to the 404 Essential Tests for IELTS
- Academic Module International Edition

Book: ISBN 0 9751832 5 7
Book & Audio CD: ISBN 0 9751832 8 1

Study Guide to the 404 Essential Tests for IELTS
- General Training Module International Edition

Book: ISBN 0 9751832 6 5
Book & Audio CD: ISBN 0 9751832 9 X

Cassette (same for both Study Guides): ISBN 0 9751832 7 3

FOR TEACHERS WHO REQUIRE AN IN-DEPTH ANALYSIS OF THE TESTS

Available at leading bookshops and direct from http://www.aapress.com.au

"*101 Helpful Hints for IELTS*" is actually two books - one for each IELTS Module - Academic or General Training. Both include two practice Listening and Speaking Tests, four Reading and Writing Tests, and an extensive Help Section, covering all four sub-tests of the IELTS examination. The unique format of the books enables students to complete the first practice test and review their performance before attempting the next test. This is achieved by linking each hint to the appropriate pages of each test, so that students can identify problem areas and understand why they may have made errors. The tests increase in difficulty as students progress through the book.

Audio CD

Cassette

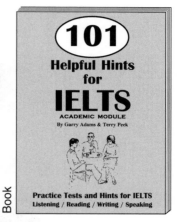

Book

101 Helpful Hints for IELTS are comprehensive course books for use in the classroom or self-study.

Academic Module	International Edition	General Training Module	International Edition
Book:	*ISBN 0 9587604 6 2*	*Book:*	*ISBN 0 9587604 9 7*
Cassette:	*ISBN 0 9578980 0 2 **	*Cassette:*	*ISBN 0 9578980 0 2 **
Book & Audio CDs(2):	*ISBN 0 9578980 7 X*	*Book & Audio CDs(2):*	*ISBN 0 9578980 9 6*

* the listening test is the same for both Modules of the test

Audio CDs

Cassette

Book

"*202 Useful Exercises for IELTS*" is our IELTS practice workbook, designed to give students of English extensive and guided IELTS examination practice. It is also a very effective learning aid for migrants and students taking EFL Secondary School Preparation Courses.

The book is divided into 5 sections, each focussing on a topic relevant to the examination, and contains:

- *27 listening exercises* - 8 news items, 5 academic lectures and 3 dictations, (all with complete tapescripts)

- 5 *reading passages* - with gapfill exercises, short-answer questions, sentence, completion tasks, multiple choice, True/False questions and matching tasks

- *10 writing tasks* - with complete model answers.

The 202 exercises complement the advice given in *101 Helpful Hints for IELTS*. Also included are punctuation, spelling, grammar and vocabulary exercises. A complete Answer Key for all exercises and a comprehensive index are provided for reference.

International Edition		Australasian Edition	
Book:	*ISBN 0 9587604 7 0*	*Book:*	*ISBN 0 9587604 5 4*
Cassette:	*ISBN 0 9578980 1 0*	*Cassette:*	*ISBN 0 9578980 2 9*
Book & Audio CDs(2):	*ISBN 0 9578980 7 X*	*Book & Audio CDs(2):*	*ISBN 0 9578980 5 3*

"*404 Essential Tests for IELTS - General Training Module*" includes four complete practice tests for the General Training versions of IELTS examinations. It has been written to give candidates extensive practice with instructions, question types and content used in the actual IELTS tests and includes detailed descriptions of the four test sections.

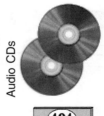

Audio CDs

Cassettes

Book

General Training Module	International Edition
Book:	*ISBN 0 9751832 3 0*
Cassettes(2):	*ISBN 0 9751832 1 4*
Book & Audio CDs(2):	*ISBN 0 9751832 4 9*

speaking writing reading

Visit our website at

http://www.aapress.com.au

and

help yourself to

FREE *IELTS PRACTICE EXERCISES*

TO **DOWNLOAD NOW**

quizzes video clips advice

NEW

IELTS 101 ONLINE COURSE
1-3 MONTHS STUDY
DETAILS AT
http://aapress.com.au/ielts101

AND MUCH MORE...

study tips

study links

forums

chat room

test your English

FAQ

'how much do you know' quiz

web polls

etc.

tips games tests audio exercises